Prophets beyond Activism

Prophets beyond Activism

Rethinking the Prophetic Roots of Social Justice

Julia M. O'Brien

WESTMINSTER
JOHN KNOX PRESS
LOUISVILLE · KENTUCKY

First edition
Published by Westminster John Knox Press
Louisville, Kentucky

24 25 26 27 28 29 30 31 32 33—10 9 8 7 6 5 4 3 2 1

Book design by Sharon Adams
Cover design by Lisa Buckley Design

Library of Congress Cataloging-in-Publication Data

Names: O'Brien, Julia M., author.
Title: Prophets beyond activism : rethinking the prophetic roots of social justice / Julia M. O'Brien.
Description: First edition. | Louisville, Kentucky : Westminster John Knox Press, [2024] | Includes bibliographical references and index. | Summary: "Challenges the common progressive narrative that the prophets of ancient Israel were primarily concerned with social justice, instead daringly offering more life-giving ways of engaging the prophetic books for the causes of justice"— Provided by publisher.
Identifiers: LCCN 2024024205 (print) | LCCN 2024024206 (ebook) | ISBN 9780664267834 (paperback) | ISBN 9781646983988 (ebook)
Subjects: LCSH: Religion and justice. | Prophets. | Justice.
Classification: LCC BL65.J87 O48 2024 (print) | LCC BL65.J87 (ebook) | DDC 261.8/3—dc23/eng/20240628
LC record available at https://lccn.loc.gov/2024024205
LC ebook record available at https://lccn.loc.gov/2024024206

Most Westminster John Knox Press books are available at special quantity discounts when purchased in bulk by corporations, organizations, and special-interest groups. For more information, please e-mail SpecialSales@wjkbooks.com.

In honor of Lancaster Theological Seminary,
and in gratitude for its generations of students, faculty,
and staff who have engaged diversity and sought justice

Contents

Introduction

The assumption that the prophets of ancient Israel were primarily concerned about social justice runs throughout the thinking and the discourse of progressive Christianity. On the websites of progressive denominations, Amos, Micah, and Isaiah are elevated as the paragons of those who critique greedy leaders, shortsighted politicians, and the coldhearted wealthy. Internet searches of "social justice" and "prophets" return dozens of articles, blogs, books, news reports, and even music that define prophets as justice warriors. Dr. Martin Luther King Jr. is a "prophet" and a "prophetic voice," as are leaders of the Black Lives Matter movement.

Closely linked with this portrayal of the Hebrew prophets is the insistence that Jesus of Nazareth was an agent of social change. According to progressives, Jesus taught and lived out a mission focused not on atonement for sin or individual piety but on uplifting the differently abled, women, queer folk, the poor, and the stranger. They depict Jesus as the successor to and ultimate realization of the prophets; the prophetic Jesus calls his followers today to be "prophetic" as well, taking up the work of the Hebrew prophets to critique the injustices of the present.

Running through such progressive descriptions of the prophets is the conviction that the true prophet stands in opposition to and apart from unjust systems of power. Prophets not only oppose kings and political officials but also priests—religious professionals who serve as gatekeepers of stifling traditions and hold fast to their own power. Unlike priests, prophets are envisioned as charismatic and often lonely individuals who courageously resist the establishment to advocate for the marginalized and critique empty religious ritual. The prophet alone stands up for justice, and "prophetic preaching" follows the lead

1

of Amos and Jesus to address social issues and adopt a countercultural stance (Turner 2008, 101; Tisdale 2010, 10–12; Ferguson 2022).

This understanding of the prophets is so common and unquestioned that I will call it an "orthodoxy"—an unquestioned and irrefutable set of beliefs whose acceptance becomes a litmus test of accurate knowledge and legitimate faith. Despite a long Christian tradition of valuing the Hebrew prophets as having predicted the coming of Jesus and despite the testimony of modern charismatics that God continues to grant special knowledge through the spiritual gifts, progressives insist that the prophets were decidedly not "foretellers" of the future with supernaturally given knowledge but rather "forthtellers" of truth that can be discerned through human, rational means. Progressives are certain not only about who the prophets *were* but also who they were obviously *not.*

This progressive orthodoxy about the prophets is a foundational assumption in myriad academic resources. Textbooks assigned in Introduction to the Hebrew Bible courses in mainline seminaries regularly instruct students that prophets did not predict the future but instead addressed "social, political, and religious circumstances in ancient Israel and Judah" (McKenzie 2009, 67). Biblical texts that *do* depict prophets as predicting the future are explained as the impositions of later editors who sought to tame the radical social justice message of the prophets (Blenkinsopp 2006, xvii–xviii, 5). Historians of early and medieval Christianity often echo this interpretation, implicitly and even explicitly "explaining" that earlier periods did not share our more enlightened views of prophets. Official church opposition to the female prophets of the second century CE Montanist movement is seen as yet another example of hierarchies silencing alternative voices (Trevett 1996), and resistance to Pentecostalism within mainline Christianity is attributed to the perennial tension between those inside and outside of institutions (Burgess 2011). These ideas have also found their way into secular sociology, as seen in descriptions of religious movements as always initiated by charismatic prophetic figures but then made rigid and bureaucratic in the second or third generations.

I am a progressive Christian. In many ways I am a rationalist, discerning truth alongside the latest advances in psychology, sociology, neuroscience, astronomy, and climate science. As a biblical scholar, I interpret biblical literature as the varied productions of human authors and attempt to understand each of the diverse testimonies within the Bible within its literary, historical, and modern contexts. And, perhaps most important to stress here, I am passionately committed to social change and critiquing systems of power. I have devoted much of my life to challenging sexism and heterosexism, and I am increasingly devoting my energies to addressing racial and environmental injustice. My progressive credentials and intentions are strong.

Yet as a scholar I am surprised by the uncontested authority of this orthodoxy as an interpretive model. Having spent my career in biblical studies, I am deeply aware of the complexity of biblical texts, the complications of reconstructing the history behind them, and the radically different conclusions that scholars can reach about them. Having studied prophetic movements from diverse times and places—from the second-century Montanists to Pentecostalism in modern Ukraine—I also have seen that responses to prophecy (as well as its very definition) vary widely. Why then is one single interpretation so widespread, treated as common knowledge, and regularly asserted without explanation or argumentation?

I am not only surprised by this interpretive orthodoxy, however. I also find it problematic. While it has inspired good work, it is neither honest nor constructive. It fails to take into consideration careful attention to the prophetic literature itself and the important modern scholarship that has illumined its origins and complications. But, more importantly, it serves to silence the voices of diverse people, too often perpetuating injustice in the name of social justice.

WHAT'S AT STAKE?

Throughout this volume, I underscore the problems with the progressive orthodoxy that the Hebrew prophets were primarily concerned with social justice.

It relies on a highly selective reading of biblical texts.

This interpretation, like all orthodoxies, prioritizes some texts over others and reads individual texts in selective ways. Regularly, for example, progressives explain that Amos and Micah count as true (classical) prophets, while Obadiah and Nahum were vengeful anonymous writers masquerading as prophets. Hosea's depiction of YHWH's love (Hos. 1) expresses a universal truth, while Hosea's description of sexual assault is mere metaphor (Hos. 2). Beloved "social justice" passages such as Amos's call to "let justice roll down like water" (Amos 5:24) and Micah's call to "do justice" (Mic. 6:8) are read as self-evident mandates for modern action, even though these texts actually say both more and less than advocates suggest. When these verses are read in their larger literary and historical contexts, they are best understood as about something quite different than modern social activists suggest.

It too often fails to consider whose justice these prophetic texts actually promote.

While they do speak of justice, prophetic texts (as all biblical texts) also are deeply embedded in the logics of racism, sexism, ethnocentrism, heterosexism, and ableism. To simply repeat their call for justice while overlooking their problematic ideologies serves to support structures of oppression. The voices of feminists, womanists, and those in postcolonial contexts challenge the view that the prophets were ethically superior forthtellers of truth, and they point to the ways in which prophetic literature casts "others" as object lessons rather than true subjects.

It emerged from a particular social and cultural context.

Despite its self-presentation as a scholarly and scientific viewpoint, the "prophets as social activists" characterization was constructed in a particular time and place for a particular set of reasons. While it rests on earlier assumptions, it congealed in nineteenth-century Germany and was popularized in the twentieth century in Great Britain and the United States. The reason that it is so ubiquitous is not that it is factually more true but because it has been advanced by "scientific" scholars and popularized by those who value those scholars. Its continued academic dominance is, in part, a reflection of the dominance of Eurocentric models of thought. Even though its language and worldview has been embraced by liberation movements in Latin America and by Black liberation theology (today in the Black Lives Matter movement), its legacy of Enlightenment rationalism and inherent racism continues to permeate its usage. Without knowing where these ideas come from, why they were formulated, and the problems they caused in the past, we ignore these legacies and, at times, perpetuate them.

It is "insider speech."

The assumption that everyone understands the discourse used by progressives is woefully misguided. For almost thirty years, I taught in an intentionally ecumenical seminary, spoken (and listened) to diverse congregations and denominational groups, and stayed current with modern religious discourse. I can confidently report that not everyone agrees on what the word "prophetic" means. When I speak about the prophets in diverse settings, I must always begin with a cross-cultural translation: explaining to those coming out of Pentecostal and related traditions what progressives are talking about, and explaining to progressives that for other streams of Christianity, "prophetic" means something quite different. In my Introduction to the Hebrew Bible classroom, this translation exercise has always been met with genuine shock. Students who thought they knew one another incredulously ask: Really? You really believe that? Even among students who share a commitment to social justice, the word "prophetic" varies in meaning.

It is intellectually arrogant.

Like any orthodoxy, the progressive orthodoxy about the prophets too easily dismisses other legitimate perspectives. It casts Pentecostals who understand prophecy as a gift of the spirit and traditionalists who define prophecy as prediction as superstitious, charlatans, mentally ill, or (using the ultimate liberal criticism) "uneducated." In some periods, it's been described as "scientific." Such dogmatism doesn't provide a helpful framework for responding to the incredibly diverse ways that prophecy is being described in various movements today, and at a more individual level, its either/or thinking often makes it difficult for people to recognize the complexity of the actual process they themselves use in evaluating the truth of competing claims about God's intention for the world.

It promotes progressive biblical ventriloquism.

One of the biggest criticisms that progressives make against conservatives is that "they" invoke the authority of the Bible for their own agendas. After working for almost forty years in progressive circles, I can affirm that progressives do the same, though with a different agenda. When the prophets are characterized as "just like" the modern social activist, the implied authority of the Bible serves to bolster one's own authority (even if implicitly). I call this tendency "biblical ventriloquism," a phrase I adapted from Craig Martin, who describes the ways that such projecting of one's values onto the Bible "exploits this authority to further various social agendas, and in doing so, maintains and reinforces that very authority" (Martin 2009, 6.8).

It promotes cognitive dissonance.

Many progressives who have been taught that the Hebrew prophets were paragons of social justice also participate in religious traditions that frame the prophetic tradition in other ways. This is particularly true for Christian bodies that observe liturgical seasons such as Advent and Lent, when lectionaries and musical selections frame the prophets as predicters of the future. In Advent, for example, the First Readings outlined in the Revised Common Lectionary for all three liturgical cycles (Years A, B, and C) are taken from the prophetic literature, often paired with Gospel texts that invite a prediction-fulfillment interpretation, such as the textual resonances between Isaiah 40:1–11 and Mark 1:1–8 that mention a voice in the wilderness in the Second Sunday of Advent in Year B. The orthodoxy that the prophets were social activists often fades away when the faithful are faced with the lectionary and the hymns of the season such as "O Come, O Come Emmanuel."

As I explore more fully in my discussion of Jeremiah in chapter 8, readers face a different kind of cognitive dissonance when they read extended passages of prophetic books rather than carefully curated selections such as in the lectionary. The progressive orthodoxy ill prepares readers to engage the violence and misogyny of prophetic rhetoric.

It hinders us from engaging the prophetic literature in more life-giving and justice-promoting ways.

Beyond critiquing the dominant progressive paradigm about the prophets, my goal is to suggest alternative ways that reading the prophetic texts can advance the work of justice. When we stop insisting that the prophets were transparent advocates for social justice, we can be open to the range of possibilities that they offer for modern advocacy. Those who care about a world rife with renewed attacks on the dignity of women and transgender persons, violent racism being given rhetorical and legal legitimacy, and the destruction of our planet now underway due to environmental harm caused by humans can no longer rely on outdated progressive tropes. We need to engage our biblical traditions fearlessly and humbly, seeking resources and inspiration as we face the present crises of our world.

To borrow the words of Second Isaiah, it is time to allow God to work in us to do "a new thing" (Isa. 43:19). I firmly believe the Bible can be a valuable companion and resource for helping humanity adapt and thrive within a future that will not look like the past—but only if we interpret it in a way that speaks the truth about biblical texts and requires us to speak in our own voices.

I intend this exploration to challenge academics and religious progressives to recognize our role in receiving and perpetuating common knowledge rather than using the text or "science" to amplify our own voices. I hope this study also spurs nonreligious folks to get honest about their own assumptions and the ways in which they cross the very boundaries used to deny other people's claims of truth. By engaging the biblical prophets in a way that goes beyond categorical and often condescending characterizations of the Hebrew prophets and the prophetic Jesus as "just like us," I seek to promote greater justice for these texts and for the inhabitants of Earth.

MAPPING THE WORK AHEAD

The book is organized into two main parts. In part 1, four chapters advance my argument that the characterization of the Hebrew prophets as social activists is not the most obvious, or even most honest, interpretation of the texts we have. Focusing on historical context, chapter 1 explores recent scholarship on the history of prophets and the prophetic books, particularly newer studies of ancient Near Eastern prophecy and of the complex layers of editing by which the prophetic books were produced. This scholarship suggests the various roles that ancient prophets played in their own settings, including the role as predicters of what YHWH intended for the future, and it underscores that editors have crafted the portrait of the prophets in ways that supported their own rhetorical goals. Chapter 2 explores just how complicated it is to understand and discern what these books actually say. When read carefully, the meaning of much prophetic poetry is obscure; when read alongside interpreters of diverse racial, gender, and other social locations, its message is not transparently one of liberatory justice for all.

Chapter 3 traces the origins and popularization of the "prophets as social critics" orthodoxy through the Enlightenment, German biblical scholarship, Romanticism, the Social Gospel, and twentieth-century liberation movements. Rather than an objective articulation of who the prophets really were, the perception that the Hebrew prophets were primarily agents of social change was created in a particular theological, intellectual, and cultural matrix. Chapter 4 draws together my conclusions from part 1 and names what I see as the dangers of the progressive insistence that the prophets were the spokespersons for social change. Failing to take seriously the complexity of these books and the characters they describe not only serves to appropriate biblical authority for one's own cause but also obscures the dynamics of power that silences other voices.

In part 2, I offer alternative readings of the Prophets for the sake of justice. Relying on the grounding in part 1, each chapter addresses a dimension of social justice and then offers case studies of key prophetic texts most commonly cited in support. In choosing the case studies, I've prioritized passages found in the Revised Common Lectionary, which I note, and I often explain how the lectionary handles these passages. After demonstrating the shortcomings of forcing these texts into the social justice mold, each chapter then suggests alternative ways of engaging the Prophets in the cause of justice while acknowledging their (and our) shortcomings. These texts do not have to be mirrors of our own views to enrich our justice engagements in the present. We can avoid biblical ventriloquism without abandoning our own commitments.

The chapters in part 2 are intentionally sequenced but may be read in any order. Chapter 5 focuses on economic justice, using Amos 8:4–7 and Micah 2:1–5 as case studies. Far from clarion calls to address poverty and economic inequality, these passages are open to diverse interpretations and diverse evaluations by readers. Chapter 6 takes up the assumption that the prophets mirrored the modern progressive concern with structural change, in conversation with the beloved passages of Amos 5:21–24 and Micah 6:1–8. It suggests ways that we can value the inspirational value of prophetic rhetoric despite its failure to chart a path of systemic reform. Chapter 7 raises questions about the inclusivity of the prophetic visions of justice, turning to Isaiah 2, Isaiah 58, and Isaiah 61 (with a nod to Luke 4). Recognizing whose needs and aspirations are ignored in these hopes for the future invites investigation of who is excluded from modern progressive justice campaigns. In chapter 8, the progressive valorization of the lone prophetic voice comes face-to-face with the details of the book of Jeremiah (especially Jer. 1:4–10 and 8:18–9:1). In this powerful yet troublesome book, we hear less the courageous countercultural voice of an individual than the theological wrestling of a traumatized community. Chapter 9 addresses climate justice throughout an engagement of the creation theology of Second Isaiah (with some attention to Gen. 1–3 and Isa. 6). Given the precarious fate of human and nonhuman life on this planet, an in-depth and honest reading of the ways in which the Bible addresses Earth and its underlying ideologies is desperately needed. No simplistic appeal to the beauty of creation and nature is adequate in our current situation of planetary devastation. The words of judgment may be more relevant in the present than paeans to the beauty of nature. In the book's conclusion, I draw together the threads of the volume and share my hopes for the future.

A few explanations are in order. Unless otherwise noted, direct citations from the Bible are from the *New Revised Standard Version Updated Edition* (NRSVue), including its references to the deity as LORD. When describing the deity apart from citations, I have tried to balance an accurate reflection of the ideology reflected in biblical texts with an attempt to avoid perpetuating gendered stereotypes. In paraphrases of biblical passages, I tend to use YHWH for the god of ancient Israel, retaining the related masculine pronouns when they are needed to underscore the text's perspective. My choice not to smooth out the ancient divine name by adding vowels, I hope, leaves the name a little jarring—as a reminder of the distance between ancient and modern understandings of the Divine. When I speak more generally about the One whom modern Christians profess, I refer to God in gender-inclusive ways.

I am deeply aware that the discourse about prophecy that I explore is not exclusive to Christians but shared by many progressive Jews. For example, the documentary *Spiritual Audacity* showcases the life and work of Rabbi Abraham Joshua Heschel, a profound scholar of the Prophets and deeply engaged social activist (Doblmeier 2021). In describing Heschel's bold confrontation of racism, anti-Semitism, and militarism, the commentators being interviewed repeatedly describe him as "prophetic" and "a prophet," without explaining their own definition of those terms. But because I am deeply, though of course never adequately, sensitive to Christian anti-Judaism, I have chosen in this volume to speak primarily from within the Christian tradition. The Jewish use of these terms and motifs is not mine to critique. For similar reasons, I refer to the Hebrew Bible when describing the sacred texts that Christians and Jews share, though when talking about Christian attitudes toward the material, I may call it the Old Testament.

Similarly, I have chosen not to critique other orthodoxies about the prophets, which come with their own internal contradictions and problematic discourse. Parallel studies of the discourse of prophecy in Pentecostalism, global charismatic movements, and political parties might also explore their dynamics, dangers, and shortcomings. My work here is to challenge my own tradition and to engage a conversation that helps it move forward. I am a progressive talking to progressives about what we can do better.

This is a wide-ranging volume. It interweaves careful readings of biblical texts within their literary and historical contexts; gives attention to the voices of feminist, womanist, and postcolonial voices; and engages with contemporary thought, such as trauma theory and intersectional analysis of the climate crisis. It is not a comprehensive study but one that seeks out broad sources of wisdom. I've attempted to share not only my own insights but also to provide readers an accessible way to learn what the technical studies of others are teaching us. In this moment of human and nonhuman suffering, the world needs all the knowledge and humility that we collectively can muster. In what follows, I offer my contribution, even as I trust that others will add their wisdom for the sake of the future.

PART ONE

Troubling the Progressive Orthodoxy about the Prophets

1

Reading the Prophets
in Historical Context

In the introduction, I explained that the goal of part 1 is to explore the origins and problems of the "prophets were social critics" orthodoxy. To do so, I need to establish that it is not the only—or even the most obvious—interpretation, especially when it comes to the Bible.

In the next two chapters, I highlight some recent developments in the study of the prophetic books of the Hebrew Bible and suggest how they destabilize any orthodoxy about the prophets. Chapter 2 explores how contemporary scholars attending to gender, race, and class distinctions are responding to the complex literary style of the prophetic books in very different ways. But first, chapter 1 begins with the past: focusing on historical considerations, it explores what we do and don't know about prophecy in the ancient Mediterranean world, as well as the long and complicated process by which the accounts of biblical prophets were composed, edited, and transmitted.

PROPHETS AS DIVINERS

Over the past one hundred years, there has been a wealth of studies of ancient documents from ancient Israel's Mesopotamian neighbors. Finds of particular interest to those who study prophecy emerge from two archaeological sites: Mari, a city-state on the Euphrates River in what is now eastern Syria, and Nineveh, at one time the capital of the Assyrian Empire and now in Mosul, Iraq. These documents attest to a range of religious professionals trained to discern clues to divine activity. One type of professional observed and interpreted various phenomena such as the flight patterns of birds and the shape of the entrails of sacrificed animals. Mesopotamian scribes also recorded the dates of eclipses, the color of the moon, and prevailing winds out of the belief that these movements were signs of divine activity. These professionals are often called "technical diviners" or "inductive diviners," since they interpret phenomena following an accepted set of procedures.

The Mari and Nineveh documents also describe another way of discerning divine intention, one that did not require physical objects. In these cases, individuals are described as receiving communication from the gods audibly or through dreams and visions or both. This "intuitive divination" or "noninductive divination" was received by diverse people and relayed to authorities, usually the king. From Mari, we have primarily administrative correspondence addressed to a king named Zimri-Lim (eighteenth century BCE) who received reports of technical divination, including the reading of the organs of sacrificial animals (known as "extispicy"). He also was informed of the divine messages communicated to cult officials who sometimes spoke in ecstasy on behalf of the gods, often while standing in front of their cult statues. Other figures seem to be professional prophets employed by the court who relayed to the king messages from other diviners around the kingdom. Many centuries later from Nineveh, we have various testimonies to divination during the reigns of the kings Assurbanipal and Esarhaddon (seventh century BCE). Esarhaddon's archives preserve reports of individual intuitive diviners as well as gathered collections of oracles. Other documents such as letters, administrative documents, word lists, and royal inscriptions refer to divination as well.

The Mari and Nineveh documents both reflect a worldview in which gods are assumed to be responsible for (almost) everything that happens. Because the gods could act in ways of their choosing, individuals (and especially kings) sought to stay in positive relationship with the gods through offerings and various ritual acts. These documents do not reflect a belief, however, that humans could control divine activity. The defeat of a city or the ravaging of a famine might be precipitated by a battle between deities or simply a decree of the divine council that the time had come. Because the gods were unpredictable, diviners at Mari sought any possible clues to what the gods might be doing.

When these documents were first studied, it was common to draw sharp contrasts between these "diviners" and Israel's "prophets": *their* diviners were dismissed as lackeys to ancient monarchs who went looking for truth in animal entrails, while *Israel's* prophets were praised as standing up to kings and who had been compelled against their will to proclaim the "word of the LORD." Recent study, however, has challenged these contrasts, many of which were produced by the desire to portray Israelite prophecy as unique.

When the accounts of the Hebrew prophets are read alongside documents from ancient Mesopotamia, numerous similarities become evident. This is especially true for the prophetic figures depicted in the books of Samuel and

Kings. For example, King Saul is described as overcome by prophetic ecstasy (1 Sam. 10:10–13); and when the prophet Elisha is sick, he lays his hands on King Joash's hands and tells him to shoot an arrow to determine God's will for a battle (2 Kgs. 13:15–19). Like their Mesopotamian counterparts, biblical prophets speak in the style of the messenger ("Thus says the LORD"). And prophets in Samuel through Kings, like diviners at Mari and Nineveh, sometimes support kings. While most folks remember that the prophet Nathan criticized King David for his taking of Uriah's wife (2 Sam. 12), they pay less attention to the fact that both of the prophets Samuel and Nathan anointed kings (1 Sam. 16; 1 Kgs. 1) and that Nathan just happened to be in the royal court when David had questions about building the Temple (2 Sam. 7)

Other similarities between the Mesopotamian and biblical texts appear as well. In both cultures, prophecies seem to have been collected in writing, perhaps for later consultation. Some of the tablets in the archives of Assyrian king Esarhaddon seem to be oracle collections, and there is some evidence that these prophetic repositories were used to test new prophetic utterances (Stökl 2015); these collections don't form a "canon" like the Bible, but they do seem to have been consulted for clues to discern a pattern with what the gods have said in various circumstances. This may be a similar idea as reflected in the book of Isaiah, where Isaiah's disciples are told to "bind up the testimony" for a later time (Isa. 8:16; 29:11–12). In addition, in testimonies from both Nineveh and the Bible, the "meaning" of a prophetic utterance isn't straightforward but often relies on wordplay, one often more noticeable to someone reading the oracle than to someone hearing it. For example, in Amos 8, the fruit (the word in Hebrew is pronounced *qayitz*) forebodes the end (pronounced *qetz*). The connection between the sign and the meaning is one revealed by the letters.

Although these cultures are often ridiculed as superstitious and gullible for believing in divination, neither ancient Mesopotamia nor ancient Israel seems to have accepted the reports of diviners uncritically. At Mari, numerous reports about the transmission of a divine message (intuitive divination) advise the king to "have an omen taken" (technical divination), presumably to cross-check the message. In addition, sometimes oracles are simply ignored. Jack Sasson tells of the case in which Zimri-Lim received three different interpretations of an oracle that mentioned "water beneath straw." Unable to determine the accurate interpretation, the king chose not to act on the information at all, which turned out to be a good decision (Sasson 1995). We can see the same kind of discernment reflected in biblical accounts in which the prophetic hero faces opposing prophets. In 1 Kings 18, the prophet Elijah singlehandedly competes with 450 prophets of the god Baal, and in 1 Kings 22, the king of Israel consults 400 prophets who predict success in battle before hearing from the prophet Micaiah ben Imlah, who predicts Israel's defeat. Amos clashes with the priest Amaziah (Amos 7), and Jeremiah faces the opposition not only of the king (Jer. 36) but also of a prophet who offers contrary political advice (Jer. 28). The opposing prophets are often depicted by readers as "false prophets," but the biblical texts often use the same Hebrew term for all the figures in the controversy. As in the case of Zimri-Lim's decision about whose interpretation of "water beneath straw" to accept, Israelite kings and even a "man of God" (1 Kgs. 13) must discern whether claims made in the name of the divine should be honored.

In the biblical accounts that I've highlighted so far, Israelite prophets are not primarily teachers of morality and do not address social inequities. As do their counterparts at Mari and Nineveh, they advise kings and discern divine truth by interpreting signs. They deliver divine messages explaining what will soon happen and why, and in this way they serve as agents of foretelling the future.

It is worth noting, however, that ancient descriptions of prophecy don't simply match the perspective of those today who believe that prophets function as predicters. Both the ancients and modern folks might believe in the possibility of foretelling the future, but the underlying belief systems may differ. Ancient Israel shared with ancient Mesopotamia (and almost all cultures prior to the Enlightenment) a worldview in which "supernatural" was not an operative category; after all, calling something "supernatural" implies that there is something that is "natural," explainable in ways other than by divine activity. Today, even those who believe that a deity (or deities) can interrupt the normal course of events usually also assume that *most of the time* events happen for more mundane, predictable, "natural" reasons. Rocks fall because of gravity; a cut gets infected due to bacteria; the movement of the stars follows the predictable pattern of the ecliptic. Societies in the ancient Near East did not share these modern assumptions. Different from most folks today, the question for ancient prophets was not *whether* God was at work but *why* YHWH was acting in particular ways. The ancient prophets are portrayed as predicting, but what they predict and how they predict is very dependent on ancient understandings of the world.

PROPHETIC BOOKS AS REDACTED

While the documents from Mari and Nineveh come from the archives of only a few kings and were frozen in time, the biblical texts were preserved, edited, interpreted, and translated over many centuries. Perhaps the most influential development in recent scholarship on the prophetic literature has been the study of how the material changed over time, called redaction criticism. Although in today's usage "redaction" usually refers to the deletion of inconvenient content, in the case of biblical literature it encompasses much more, including the modification and addition of content by editors. It was once common to try to undo these edits, to retrieve what the prophets really said from the tampering of later editors, so as to retrieve the "historical" Jeremiah or Amos. More recently, however, the interest has turned to reading the books within the context of their redactors, trying to understand what the book may have meant to those who put it into the book we have.

Increasingly, the time period being proposed for most of the redaction of the prophetic books is the postexilic period. "Postexilic" refers to the situation in the land of Israel around 550–350 BCE, when the descendants of Judeans who had been exiled by the Babylonian Empire returned to their ancestral lands under the auspices of the Persian Empire. As described in the biblical books of Ezra and Nehemiah, these returning groups understood their efforts as a restoration of the Judah that had existed prior to the Babylonian destruction of Jerusalem in 586 BCE. They sought to rebuild not only infrastructure such as Jerusalem's Temple and its protective walls but also their self-understanding in relationship to their deity. They sought to understand why the kingdoms of Israel and Judah had fallen and to find hope for the future.

Read as retrospective theology, the prophetic materials serve precisely this function. They defend the justice of YHWH, insisting that both Israel and Judah fell because they failed to heed the message sent from YHWH through the prophets. And they offer hope that their changing fortunes might signal divine forgiveness. When read as productions of the Persian period, the books are not simple transcripts or biographies but retrospective and profoundly theological documents in which prophets discern the divine perspective on the truth of the past and the future.

Deuteronomy and Joshua–Kings

There are actually two collections of prophetic materials. One includes the books of Joshua, Judges, Samuel, and Kings, which are primarily narrative in style and tell stories about prophets such as Elijah, Elisha, and Nathan. In Judaism, these books are called the Former Prophets; in Christianity, they are included among the historical books. These books so closely mirror the vocabulary and outlook of the book of Deuteronomy that most scholars believe that they were edited to *show* the theology that Deuteronomy *tells*, hence their designation as the Deuteronomistic History.

In Deuteronomy, prophets are judged by two criteria. Deuteronomy 18:22 lists accuracy of prediction as essential: "If a prophet speaks in the name of the LORD but the thing does not take place or prove true, it is a word that the

LORD has not spoken. The prophet has spoken it presumptuously; do not be frightened by it." Yet prophecy also must adhere to Deuteronomy's key theological claim that Israel must worship YHWH alone. Even if prophets predict accurately, they should be put to death if they encourage worship of other gods (Deut. 13:1–5). Deuteronomy insists that if Israel honors YHWH exclusively, they will prosper; if Israel turns to other gods, they will not live long in the land (Deut. 30:19).

The books of the Deuteronomistic History were edited to show exactly that outcome: whenever Israel failed to worship YHWH alone, it fell to its enemies. In the book of Judges, a series of military failures is attributed to YHWH's anger for Israel's worship of other gods (e.g., Judg. 2:11–15), and according to 2 Kings the nation of Judah went into exile because of its idolatry. Throughout these books, the prophets behave in a very "Deuteronomic" way. In 2 Kings 9, the Israelite queen Jezebel is killed in the exact way the prophet Elisha had foretold in 1 Kings 21:23. "True" prophets also insist on obedience to YHWH's commands. Elijah's success over the rival prophets of Baal is attributed to his claims that YHWH alone is Lord and that Elijah has acted according to YHWH's command (1 Kgs. 18:36). Earlier in 1 Kings, a "man of God" is killed because he did not keep "the commandment that the LORD your God commanded you" (1 Kgs. 13:21). The prophet Micaiah ben Imlah offers a contrary message than the majority of "false prophets" because he insists, "Whatever the LORD says to me, that I will speak" (1 Kgs. 22:14).

These books of the Deuteronomistic History explain Israel's and Judah's exile as punishment for failing to obey YHWH's commandments, despite the warnings of the prophets:

> Yet the Lord warned Israel and Judah by every prophet and every seer, saying, "Turn from your evil ways and keep my commandments and my statutes, in accordance with all the law that I commanded your ancestors and that I sent to you by my servants the prophets." (2 Kgs. 17:13)

Throughout its history, claims the Deuteronomistic History, prophets alerted the people to the importance of obedience to worship of YHWH alone and the dire consequences for failure. But the people did not listen. This teaching of the prophets is clear and consistent—thanks to the redactors.

Prophetic Books

No less than the Deuteronomistic History, the books known by Jews as the Latter Prophets and by Christians as the Prophets have gone through extensive editing. Although interpreters often speak of the distinct personality of these prophets (such as Jeremiah, Isaiah, and Hosea), several centuries of scholarship have highlighted how complex these books really are and how carefully they have been composed.

Some clues of redaction are easy to recognize, such as the fact that the prophets' actions are usually narrated in third person and the opening verses of each book (called "superscriptions") explicitly state that what follows are words *about* the prophet rather than *by* him. Other clues are more subtle but also clearly indicate that these books do not provide clear windows into the prophetic figures they describe. Major time shifts are evident—for example, in the book of Isaiah where early chapters announce pending divine judgment by the Assyrians in the eighth century BCE and later chapters describe the imminent actions of the sixth-century Persian king Cyrus. Similar jumps in time and tone are found between Micah 3 and 4 and Zechariah 8 and 9. Amos ends with a concern about the restoration of the Davidic monarchy (Amos 9), quite out of keeping with the rest of the book. The book of Jeremiah looks so different in the Hebrew text (on which most English translations are based) than in the ancient Greek translation known as the Septuagint that some scholars think two different versions of the book must have circulated for a long time. Many scholars of the Minor Prophets—the twelve small books found at the end of the collection—find evidence of editing between and within books to fashion them into a single Book of the Twelve. For example, the book of Amos opens with the same phrase (Amos 1:2) found at the end of the previous book of Joel (Joel 3:16): "The LORD roars from Zion." Themes such as the Day of YHWH introduced in the first book develop as the collection unfolds.

In their final forms, most of the Latter Prophets are postexilic explanations of why Israel and Judah had fallen. They are *theodicies*—defenses of YHWH's justice in carrying out this punishment. In these writings (as in the Deuteronomistic History), prophets are portrayed as spokespersons for such a theology: prophets had warned Israel and Judah of the consequences of their failure to observe YHWH's commandments. This message is clearly articulated in the Persian-period book of Zechariah:

> Do not be like your ancestors, to whom the former prophets proclaimed, "Thus says the LORD of hosts, return from your evil ways and from your evil deeds." But they did not hear or heed me. . . . My words and my statutes, which I commanded my servants the prophets, did they not overtake your ancestors? (Zech. 1:4–6)

For these postexilic writers, the redactors, the reminder that earlier prophets had warned Israel of the consequences of its behavior also served a hopeful purpose for their own time: the justified punishment of Jerusalem could be seen as now accomplished, such that the present community could thrive if it avoided the mistakes of its ancestors.

Reading these books from the vantage point of their postdestruction readers, we can clearly recognize their attempts to respond to the trauma of the Babylonian invasion of Jerusalem. As I explain more fully in chapter 8, this observation allows us to read the book of Jeremiah in light of trauma studies; its expressions of anger, grief, and abjection, as well as its visions of YHWH violently punishing a feminized Jerusalem, reflect a community's attempt to retell its experience "slant," to process its trauma by reliving through refracted literary means (O'Connor 2011). Such a retrospective lens helps us consider, too, the import of the stories of Jeremiah's conflict with another prophet, Hananiah. In Jeremiah 28, Hananiah prophesies the end of hostilities and the restoration of Judah's king, while Jeremiah prophesies continued devastation and "remembers" that earlier prophets had prophesied war, famine, and pestilence. Jeremiah is proven to be the "true prophet," not only in the closing verses of the chapter but also in the historical memory of the survivors. Because ancient and modern readers know that Jeremiah had been right, they not only sympathize with this reluctant prophet but also accept the theology advanced by Persian-period scribes: prior to Jerusalem's fall, YHWH had warned the people through true prophets, but they heeded false prophets instead.

The Cumulative Effect

In their current forms, the books of the Deuteronomistic History and the Latter Prophets are connected to one another. An almost identical story about Isaiah and Hezekiah appears in Isaiah 39 and 2 Kings 20; Jeremiah 52 and 2 Kings 24 share an account of the fall of Jerusalem. Moreover, the opening superscriptions of the prophetic books clearly follow the historical chronology of the Deuteronomistic History. When the Deuteronomistic History and the Latter Prophets are read together, they present an unbroken chain of prophets from Moses to Malachi who warned the people of pending disaster. This understanding of prophecy would have served a national narrative that attributed the Babylonian destruction to bad leaders and unfaithful Israelites rather than divine failure.

Redaction not only links the Deuteronomistic History and the Latter Prophets but also integrates both with the conception that divine will is mediated through the Torah—the law of Moses recorded in a book. The Persian-period books of Ezra and Nehemiah (Ezra 7:11; Neh. 8) speak of this "book of the law," which is at least some version of the first five books of the Jewish and Christian Bibles. This focus on written documents as repositories of divine will in turn appears in redactions made in the Persian period to the Deuteronomistic History and the Latter Prophets. In a very Deuteronomistic speech, Joshua 1:8 instructs the people to live by the "book of the law," and in 2 Kings 22 the prophetess Huldah is called not to discern YHWH's will on her own but to authenticate the "book of the law" found in the Temple. In Jeremiah 36, the words of Jeremiah are delivered to the people, officials, and the king not by the prophet himself but through the reading of his words by the scribe Baruch. Redaction draws connections between Moses (the hero of the Torah) and the prophet Elijah, who also encounters YHWH at Mount Horeb / Sinai (1 Kgs. 19:8–18); and Malachi ends the Latter Prophets with an appeal to remember Moses's teaching and to prepare for Elijah's return (Mal. 4:4–5).

WHY REDACTION MATTERS

Redaction criticism problematizes any categorical claims about who the ancient prophets actually were and what they actually did. It stresses that accounts of prophetic actions and speeches are not simple windows into the work of heroic individuals but rather highly crafted literary productions of communities seeking to understand the workings of YHWH and thereby to find a way forward from disaster.

Some scholars have attempted to preserve the view that the prophets were concerned with social action by prioritizing the layers of the text prior to the postexilic redaction. Redaction critics in the late nineteenth and early twentieth centuries, for example, dismissed these changes to the text as attempts to control the disruptive reality of the prophets. The historical prophets, they argued, were concerned with ethics and were opposed to religious institutions; later "pious" postexilic redactors tried to make the prophets into something else. One more recent example of this type of argument is that of Joseph Blenkinsopp, who argues that the original "profile of the prophet as critic of social mores and powerful counterforce to corrupt political and religious elites" was obscured by postexilic redactors but properly restored in the modern period (Blenkinsopp 2006, xvii–xviii, 5).

Such attempts, however, are problematic. They don't recognize that it is actually redaction that highlights the prophets as lone voices criticizing their community and opposing kings and priests. The depiction of "true prophets" such as Jeremiah and Micaiah ben Imlah as isolated individuals who stood up to multitudes of "false prophets" is just as much of a construction of the prophetic role as any other. This depiction was crafted to support postexilic theological claims that the nation fell because it followed its misguided leaders instead of listening to YHWH's prophets.

At the same time, redaction also deserves credit for highlighting the role of the prophets as predicters of the future. If the prophetic books were crafted into their current forms by those who had already experienced destruction, then the straight line between prophetic prediction and fulfillment is one drawn by a redactor, a connection that also serves a theological purpose. If readers might believe that the prophetic warnings of disaster had come true in the past, those living after the disaster might also believe that the prophetic words of hope would now materialize. Both views of the prophets—as foretellers and forthtellers—are the accomplishments of redactors.

DISAGREEMENTS ABOUT PROPHECY

There is another plank to my argument that prophecy doesn't fit any orthodoxy, and it is grounded in the biblical text itself: people have always disagreed about prophecy because claims about prophecy are always connected with wider beliefs and worldviews.

It would be easy to overlook the Bible's disagreements about prophecy. This was one of the big successes of the redactors of the Deuteronomistic History and the Latter Prophets. By presenting prophets as those who relayed divine messages about pending events and who warned communities of the punishment for not following the commandments of YHWH, the redactors lulled us into believing that there is one "biblical" take on prophecy. And by claiming that redaction tried to hide the truth of the prophets, some interpreters want us to believe that there is only one other truth about prophecy. But paying close attention to how prophecy is discussed suggests that not all biblical writers thought about prophecy in the same way—even writers working in the same time period.

This contested nature of prophecy can clearly be seen within and between various biblical writings from the Persian period. A fascinating example is the book of Nehemiah, which describes the rebuilding efforts of those who returned to Jerusalem from Babylon in the fifth century BCE. On the one hand, Nehemiah reflects the prophets-as-warners interpretation we've been discussing:

> [Our ancestors] were disobedient and rebelled against you [O YHWH] and cast your law behind their backs and killed your prophets, who had warned them in order to turn them back to you, and they committed great blasphemies. (Neh. 9:26)

On the other hand, Nehemiah 6 describes a series of conflicts in which prophets of Nehemiah's own time are involved. Sanballat, an adversary, is described as accusing Nehemiah of drumming up prophets to declare the return of the monarchy, and Nehemiah is himself in conflict with the prophet Shemaiah. When Shemaiah predicts an attempt on Nehemiah's life, Nehemiah discerns that the prophet was not sent by YHWH but only prophesied for money (Neh. 6:12). Without discrediting the possibility that the prophet might indeed foresee the future, Nehemiah is portrayed as a leader with powerful foes but gifts of discernment more powerful than those of prophets. This fits the purpose of the book: to bolster the reputation of its lead character. Clearly, the book's *talk about* prophecy doesn't match *real-life struggles* over prophecy.

Comparing Persian-period books shows other differences as well. Joel, which laments the devastation that the community is now facing, includes in its extravagant promises for a utopian future a vision of (almost) everyone acting as a prophet. YHWH proclaims,

> I will pour out my spirit on all flesh;
> your sons and your daughters shall prophesy,
>   your old men shall dream dreams,
>   and your young men shall see visions.
> Even on the male and female slaves,
> in those days, I will pour out my spirit.
>   Joel 2:28–29

In contrast, the second section of the book of Zechariah, likely written in a similar time, shuts down the possibility of future prophecy:

> If any prophets appear again, their fathers and mothers who bore them will say to them, "You shall not live, for you speak lies in the name of the LORD"; and their fathers and their mothers who bore them shall pierce them through when they prophesy. On that day the prophets will be ashamed, every one, of their visions when they prophesy; they will not put on a hairy mantle in order to deceive. (Zech. 13:3–4)

For Joel, the prediction of universal prophecy helps advance its claim of the extravagance of divine promises. In contrast, Zechariah expresses the desire for a Davidic king and shuts down prophecy to do so.

Perhaps the most interesting Persian-period view of prophecy is found in the book of Chronicles. Written at least a generation after the Deuteronomistic History, Chronicles takes the stories found in Joshua through Kings and reframes them for a new generation. The stories about David found in 2 Samuel, for example, are refashioned to downplay David's faults and to give him more credit for the organization of worship in the Jerusalem Temple. In its description of prophets, Chronicles goes further than the Deuteronomistic History in downplaying miracle working as a prophetic action: none of the miracles of Elijah described in 1 Kings appear in Chronicles, and Elisha is completely missing. In addition, Chronicles expands and adds explanatory speeches to characterize prophets as interpreters of events.

Chronicles also introduces another aspect to our understanding of divine communication with humans in ancient Israel: those given the label "prophet" are not the only ones who have access to divine inspiration. Chronicles does not use the label "prophet" for anyone in the Persian period, yet it depicts a whole cadre of its contemporaries as inspired/overcome by the "spirit of the LORD." For example,

> Then the spirit of the LORD came upon Jahaziel son of Zechariah, son of Benaiah, son of Jeiel, son of Mattaniah, a Levite of the sons of Asaph, in the middle of the assembly. (2 Chron. 20:14; no Kings parallel)

The phrase "spirit of the LORD" is the same one that earlier books attribute to prophets, such as Elijah (1 Kgs. 18–19), Micaiah ben Imlah (1 Kgs. 22:24), and Ezekiel (Ezek. 11:37). In Chronicles, the spirit possesses priests, Levites, soldiers, and even a pharaoh. According to the consonants in the Hebrew text of 1 Chronicles 25:1, Temple musicians are called "prophets," though the Hebrew tradition encourages the translation "ones prophesying with their instruments."

Chronicles, it seems, recognizes the possibility of divine inspiration among those it is hesitant to label a "prophet." The distinction between calling someone a "prophet" and accepting their speech as divinely given might at times reflect a simple vocabulary shift; at other times it may reflect very different understandings of the way that YHWH communicates with humans.

In these Persian-period writings, prophecy is a trope that is employed in various ways, almost always in support of a larger ideology or theology. In Nehemiah, the characterization of Nehemiah as uncowed by prophets serves to bolster his own authority, a key theme in the book. In Joel, the promise of widespread prophecy is linked with the book's promise of glory days ahead. In (Second) Zechariah, the future belongs to a coming Davidic king from whom prophets would only be a distraction. In Chronicles, prophecy is redefined as a Temple activity so that prophecy can be tacitly honored while its authority is transferred to others.

PROPHECY BEYOND THE HEBREW BIBLE

While a full analysis of prophecy in early Judaism and early Christianity is beyond the scope of my discussion here, it's important to acknowledge that the characterization of prophecy in the Second Temple period reflects a mixture of these Near Eastern motifs with Greek and Roman thinking. Throughout the Mediterranean world in the first century, "prophecy" meant primarily prediction of the future. Such prediction could be accomplished by various means: through divination and the reading of omens, as well as through dreams and visions. This ability to discern the future was considered integral to the functioning of society. In ancient Greece and Rome, for example, mechanisms for divination were regulated by the state.

Diviners of this era also sought to predict the future by decoding clues in ancestral documents. In this process of what Annette Reed calls the "textualization of knowledge" (Reed 2017, 13), they sought clues in the words of the past for what might yet happen. They archived and pored over ancient texts not simply for the sake of remembering the past but also out of the belief that embedded in that ancestral lore were the mysteries of the future.

In Jewish and Christian texts of the Hellenistic and Roman periods, we can see such understandings of prophecy at work. For example, in the book of Daniel, one of the last books of the Hebrew Bible to have been composed, Daniel finds clues to the future in the book of Jeremiah (Dan. 9:2). Similarly, biblical commentaries from the Dead Sea Scrolls decipher books in the Hebrew Bible such as Nahum and Habakkuk as encrypted messages about their own situation.

In this era, another term that signals a discussion of prophecy is "spirit." Although "spirit" was already linked with prophecy and other inspired figures by the Persian period (as seen in the examples above from Chronicles), the association between the two terms intensifies in this period. For example, the Septuagint, the Greek translation of Hebrew texts crafted in Egypt around 200 BCE, adds "spirit" to several descriptions of the biblical prophets, such as in the Septuagint's translation of Zechariah 1:6: "which I told *in my spirit* to the prophets." Documents from the Dead Sea Scrolls characterize "the spirit" as transmitting divine truth, identifying the ones "anointed with the spirit" as the prophets.

Our awareness of how prophecy was understood in the Second Temple period can help us recognize that sometimes the legitimacy of prophecy is being debated even when the words "prophet" and "prophecy" aren't used. Sometimes debates instead are about visions, dreams, knowledge, or the interpretation of earlier texts. Moreover, in these periods prophecies might be discerned in books other than those that appear in the prophets of the Bible. Coded truths about the future might be found not only in books attributed to the prophets Isaiah and Jeremiah but also in other books, including Psalms and Genesis.

The documents now collected into the New Testament reflect many of these same dynamics. For example, when the Gospel of Matthew recounts the birth of Jesus, it depicts God communicating with the wise men and Mary's soon-to-be husband, Joseph, through dreams, and it interprets the sayings of ancient prophets such as Isaiah and Micah as predictions now fulfilled in the present (Matt. 1). The repeated insistence that the events of Jesus' life fulfilled earlier Scripture are often seen by modern people as manipulative prooftexting, but this writer shared with his era the assumption that ancient texts might contain truths yet to be discerned.

Key texts for exploring early Christian perspectives on prophecy are the books of Luke and Acts, believed by most scholars to have been written as a two-volume set by a single author (for the sake of convenience I'll call him "Luke"). In this story that runs from the birth of Jesus to the flourishing of the early church, a ubiquitous character is the Holy Spirit (which by this period, as discussed earlier, had become a term associated with prophecy). The Spirit imbues Jesus and his followers with the ability to know the future, to heal, and to discern the truth of a situation in ways that are clearly "prophetic." Moreover, what Jesus predicts in Luke often comes to fulfillment in Acts: just as Jesus predicts that his disciples will face persecutors yet be victorious over them (Luke 21:12–15), so the apostles are victorious over those who bring them to trial (Acts 4:5–17). In Acts, numerous apostles are explicitly called prophets (Acts 13:1; 15:32).

It would be difficult to overestimate the importance that the account in Acts 2 plays not only in the book but also in the thinking of later Christians. After Jesus' death and resurrection, it relates, believers in Jesus were gathered in Jerusalem at the time of the Jewish feast of Pentecost. The Spirit came upon them, allowing them to speak in different tongues that could be understood by the international crowd of visitors who were in the city for the festival. The apostle Peter explains that this outpouring of the Spirit was the fulfillment of a prophecy by the prophet Joel. Luke strengthens this prediction-fulfillment scheme by making two additions to the Greek version of Joel 2 that was Luke's Scripture: "and they shall prophesy" in Acts 2:18 and "signs" in Acts 2:19. Through these expansions, prophecy is linked not only with the Holy Spirit but also with signs and wonders. Thus, when Acts describes the apostles as doing signs and wonders (as it does repeatedly, such as in Acts 5:12 and 15:12), it is claiming that the church continues to be blessed with the gifts of prophecy. In Luke–Acts, the appearance of prophecy underscores the legitimacy of the church.

Other literature in the New Testament seems far more concerned than Luke–Acts in helping the early Christian community discern the truth of competing prophetic claims. The book of 1 Thessalonians, one of the earliest Christian writings, recognizes the need to test individual utterances: it advises, "Do not despise prophecies, but test everything" (1 Thess. 5:19–22). The early Christian texts of 1 and 2 John offer a concrete criterion for distinguishing between true and false prophecy: true prophecy confirms the church's claim that "Jesus Christ has come in the flesh" (1 John 4:2; 2 John 7). While Luke–Acts celebrates prophecy and depicts Jerusalem as killing prophets, these Christian documents that are just as early (or earlier) place controls on prophecy by advancing a creedal test for its accuracy. Like Deuteronomy before them, these writers insist that accuracy of prediction is an insufficient test of prophecy; valid prophecy must advance correct teaching. Prophecy is judged by its content.

A different type of control is placed on prophecy in 1 Corinthians 12–14, the most extensive discussion of prophecy in the New Testament. As Laura Nasrallah explains in her helpful study of early Christian responses to prophecy, Paul seeks to limit the Corinthians' self-important prophetic claims by challenging what is actually possible to know in this life (Nasrallah 2003). While the Corinthians regard themselves as superior to other Christians because of their extraordinary gifts of the spirit, especially their ability to speak in tongues, Paul insists that there is no complete knowledge of the divine in this life and that prophecy is imperfect and temporary. Although 1 Corinthians 13 is usually treated as a celebration of love, at its heart it is a polemic against exalted prophetic claims: "Love never ends. But as for prophecies, they will come to an end; as for tongues, they will cease; as for knowledge, it will come to an end. For we know only in part, and we prophesy only in part" (1 Cor. 13:8–12).

Paul's downgrading of prophecy serves the larger goal that runs throughout his writings: to prioritize the unity of the Christian community. Just as Paul seeks to downplay the difference between "Jew or Greek, slave or free . . . male and female" (Gal. 3:28) and insists that Christians behave in ways that please one's neighbor (Rom. 15:2), so too he promotes communal cohesion by deprioritizing extraordinary gifts such as prophecy.

In these examples from the New Testament, we see that claims for and against prophecy served diverse functions in the early church. While Luke–Acts celebrates prophecy as confirmation of the Christian message, Paul and other early authors recognize the problems posed by prophecy and offer criteria for its discernment. Although later interpreters often explain these different views of prophecy as chronological—moving from the most free to the most restrictive—such an easy developmental scheme doesn't fit the evidence. From the earliest days of the church, prophecy was seen as important to the degree by which it affirmed Christian claims and Christian values.

Early Christian literature from outside the Bible follows many of these themes. The Shepherd of Hermas, a text from the second century cited by many early Christians, describes itinerant Christian prophets and instructs believers to offer them food. Yet it also offers guidelines for evaluating their validity: true prophets, it claims, do not issue prophecies for hire. The Didache, likely written in the first century, also condemns itinerant prophets who stay in a town more than three days, seeking to become wealthy through their craft.

Perhaps the most debated case about Christian attitudes toward ongoing prophecy is that of the Montanists. Montanism was a Christian movement that began in the late second century in what is today Turkey, after a man named Montanus and then later two women, Maximilla and Priscilla, began to speak in ecstatic trances and proclaimed they had received a new prophecy. The movement expanded to Rome and North Africa, bringing with it new writings and new teachings, including rigorous ethical demands such as intense fasting, the dissolution of marriage, refusal of remarriage after the death of a spouse, and the veiling of virgins. We have no surviving records from the Montanists themselves, but a defense of their positions comes to us from North African church father Tertullian, who may have become a Montanist late in life; at the very least, he was a staunch ally. The Montanists did not fare well. Church councils accused them of bad theology and enacted a series of anti-Montanist legislations. In 550 CE, a church leader burned their shrine and seized their cathedral and property, effectively ending the movement.

The fate of the Montanists is frequently interpreted as evidence of those in power denying the validity of outsiders who speak in God's name, supporting the narrative that prophets are courageous voices challenging unjust systems of power. Some consider them as mistreated "pioneers of new forms of ministry" (Tabbernee 2007, 423), and numerous feminists argue that the church's real concern with Montanism was the freedom it gave women (Trevett 1996, 14, 19). Yet as in the other cases we have studied, it is helpful to read these debates about Montanism within their context. Without denying the realities of sexism and other forms of bias, it's also important to consider what else might have been at stake in these debates over prophecy.

In addition to her work on Paul, Nasrallah offers a contextual reading of the Montanist controversy and points out several important aspects of the debates. She shows that the church fathers don't speak against ongoing prophecy in general. Irenaeus, for example, opposes those (like the Montanists) who practice prophecy outside of the church, but he boasts of those within the church "who possess prophetic gifts, and who through the Spirit speak all kinds of languages, and bring to light for the general benefit the hidden things of men, and declare the mysteries of God" (*Against Heresies* 5.6.1). Another church writer, Lactantius, was willing to embrace prophecies from the surrounding Greek culture (the Sibylline Oracles) as long as they were understood as proclaiming the truth of Jesus.

As Nasrallah shows, the protests that the early church leaders make against the Montanists aren't about the fact that they claimed to prophesy but are more specific than that. One anonymous writer objects to the fact that others could not understand the prophetic utterances of Montanus, Priscilla, and Maximilla; like Paul before him, he insisted that prophecy should build up the church. Another ancient writer mounts what Nasrallah calls an epistemological argument: valuing rationality over ecstasy, this writer argues that biblical prophets were never "out of their mind" as are the New Prophets (as the Montanists were known) but always in possession of their rational faculties. This writer also critiques the Montanists' embrace of the prophetic task, since, he argues, the prophets of Scripture resisted the prophetic call.

Challenging those who interpret the church's rejection of Montanism as the attempt of a church growing in power trying to kill off voices of opposition, challenges to individual prophetic claims were not an innovation of Christian leaders in the generations after Jesus. In and outside the Bible, there had long been moves to evaluate prophecy by comparing it with traditional wisdom, often though not always recorded in written documents. In the Nineveh archives, oracle collections provided one guide to new prophecy; in Persian-period Judaism, Torah determined prophecy's truth; in the New Testament, Christian proclamations about Jesus were the benchmark for true prophecy; and in early Christianity, these proclamations and the emerging canon of Scripture became the basis—or at least the stated basis—for responding to new claims of divine communication. Similarly, the role of the community in validating prophetic claims is a dynamic that runs through all these periods. Irenaeus's insistence that prophecy must benefit the group is similar to the claims made by Paul, as in 1 Corinthians discussed earlier.

Interestingly, those who defend the Montanists usually focus on the fact that they prophesied rather than on the actual content of the prophecy that the Montanists proclaimed. While it is true that the Montanists counted women among the prophets, they also proclaimed that the Spirit dictated very rigorous controls on women's (and men's) bodies. The Montanists may have foregrounded women prophets, but their teaching was not one that most modern activists would advance.

Clearly, throughout all these cases, prophecy functions in ways that are quite different than that described by modern social activists. Prophecy is important (and dangerous) for many other reasons than its critique of structures of oppression.

CONCLUSION

The orthodoxy that the ancient Israelite prophets and their prophetic heirs were social activists doesn't hold up to historical investigation of the texts in which they are described. Parallels with other ancient Near Eastern literature and contextual studies of Greek and Roman literature underscore not only the predictive function of ancient diviners or prophets but also an ancient worldview in which all events are understood as revelatory of divine intention. Redaction criticism insists that biblical accounts of prophecy are not firsthand transcripts or (auto)biographies of Israelite teachers or preachers but instead artful compositions written by later communities.

Reading biblical texts with an eye to their historical dimensions—when they were written, how they were edited—also makes even more evident an observation that careful readers of these texts might conclude on their own: the Bible does not portray prophecy in only one way. It is common within the "prophets as activists" orthodoxy to prioritize some prophets over others: to treat Amos, Micah, and Isaiah as the "classical prophets" who embody the true nature of prophecy along with their prophetic heir Jesus and to dismiss those who came before and after as falling short of this ideal. Historical study, however, underscores that all presentations of prophecy are constructions of later communities. Amos lambasts mistreatment of the poor but he is presented doing so in a way that serves to explain why Israel fell: he "predicted" what later redactors had already experienced. We have no more access to the "historical" Amos, Isaiah, and Micah than to the real-life controversies over prophecy described in Nehemiah. Our access to the historical Jesus is likewise restricted.

In Persian-period texts as in other times and places, discourse about prophecy is never just about prophecy. It is intricately connected with worldviews and claims to authority. How does God communicate with humans? Who has access to divine will? What role do governmental and religious institutions play in discerning God's intentions? These are questions faced by ancient authors whose words addressed their own historical contexts. They are also questions that face readers of these texts, to whom the next chapter turns.

2

The Trouble with Reading

The insistence that the biblical prophets were social activists suggests that we know exactly who the prophets were and what they did. In the previous chapter I attempted to show that this kind of historical confidence is misguided. Reading biblical texts within their own historical contexts underscores that they tell us far more about the views of their authors than about the prophetic figures they portray.

In this chapter I explore other reasons why it is problematic to insist that the biblical prophets (even the classical ones) were forthtellers. First, I show that it is difficult to even know what these books *say*. Their literary style is evocative and provocative rather than straightforward and clear, complicating all attempts to distill a singular message from them. Second, I show why not all readers find the prophets to be ethical champions. Considering how these texts depict women, children, and the poor raises the question of just who benefits from prophetic speech. For my examples, I focus on the books of the Latter Prophets, exploring their distinctive style and the complications of their meaning.

PROPHETS AS POETS

While *stories* about prophetic characters appear in books such as Jeremiah and Hosea, most of the material attributed to prophets is *poetry*. Most English translations make these genre distinctions evident by formatting. A good example can be seen in the different typesetting used in the NRSVue for the speeches in Jeremiah 6 and the narrative in Jeremiah 7. This separation of prophetic poetry and prose doesn't appear in early manuscripts of the Prophets but is based instead on the scholarly judgment that these passages share many of the features of poetry found in books such as Psalms. In Hebrew, these verses often employ parallelism, in which two lines are paired to produce meaning; terseness, with verbs often absent; and repetition of key words. They also display a wide range of literary tropes that are familiar to readers of English poetry, including metaphor, simile, alliteration, assonance, hyperbole, irony, and wordplay.

Why the prophetic literature appears in poetry has been debated. As I explain further in chapter 3, in the eighteenth century the English scholar Robert Lowth claimed that the poetic nature of prophecy is evidence of its divine inspiration, the passionate outpouring from the prophet's heart. In the following decades, biblical scholars and literary critics (including Samuel Taylor Coleridge and William Blake) equated the prophet with the poet, both imagined as expressive individual geniuses. Consistently, though, even most of these interpreters assumed that prophetic style was intended to move and instruct its readers. The prophets were described as preachers or teachers who used poetry as a rhetorical device to convey a point. This interpretative trend continues in the present in sermons, commentaries, and Bible studies that seek to extract from the bewildering prophetic language the distinctive "message" of each prophet for the past and for the present.

Recent study of prophetic poetry, however, has stressed the ways in which it differs from persuasive rhetoric and persistently resists reduction to a simple point. In the words of Gerald Morris, this poetry "complicat[es] sense with sound, by using incongruous words or expressions, by deforming expected emphases or by deliberately obscuring or even contradicting itself" (Morris 1996, 42). This dimension of poetry can be seen, for example, in the ways that prophetic books employ metaphors. Sometimes, so many comparisons are used that their reference is easily lost, such as in the book of Hosea. English translations (especially the most recent ones) often smooth out the disruptions that are evident to a reader of Hebrew, but even English readers can notice the piling up of imagery in Hosea 7, where Israel is called adulterers, a heated oven, a burned cake, a silly dove, a defective bow, and babblers. One image replaces another, as if the sinfulness of Israel defies any one description. The meaning of individual metaphors in Hosea also shifts over the course of the book: in Hosea 6:4 the affections of Ephraim and Judah are compared to dew that evaporates—but the evaporation of dew in Hosea 13:3 symbolizes pending destruction, while in 14:6 the Holy One is like life-giving dew (Morris 1996, 63–69). In Hosea, dew symbolizes sin, punishment, or salvation—or all three—making it difficult to track Hosea's point.

Throughout the Latter Prophets, it's often unclear where metaphor stops and meaning begins: what's the metaphor, and what is its referent? For example, in Joel 1, scholars disagree whether invading armies are being compared to locusts, locust swarms are being compared to armies, or the book is describing two different invasions. In Micah 2:12–13, does YHWH intend good or ill by gathering the people as sheep into a pen? What are the people actually doing when Amos accuses them of "trampl[ing] the head of the poor into the dust of the earth" (Amos 2:7)—physically assaulting them or burying them in debt? Is Amos 5:21–23 a flat rejection of ritual, or is this an exaggeration to underscore the failure of ritual that is not paired with justice? Carolyn Sharp similarly points to the difficulty in agreeing what the book of Jonah is actually about. While interpreters may agree that Jonah is satire, they disagree about who—or what—is being satirized: "one critic's ironizing hyperbole may be another critic's passionate truth claim" (Sharp 2009, 130, 6). In chapter 5, I talk at greater length about the significance of these ambiguities in the books of Amos and Micah, so important to social activists.

In addition, the frequent use of puns in prophetic literature challenges the logical connection between sin and punishment that the prophets are often seen to advance. Examples are best recognized in Hebrew, such as in Amos 8:1–2, where the only connection between "summer fruit" and "the end" is the sound of the Hebrew words. In Amos 5:5, the fate of the city of Gilgal is sealed by the unfortunate similarity in sounds between its name and the Hebrew words for "surely going into exile" (*gala yigleh*). In Micah 1:10–16, the fate of cities seems dependent on the resonances of their names with particular words for punishment: the inhabitants of Beth-leaphrah (in Hebrew: "house of dust") should roll in dust (Mic. 1:10); Achzib sounds like the Hebrew word for "deception" (Mic. 1:14). Some commentators have attempted to explain this listing of towns on historical grounds, yet in Micah's poetry the specificity of these locations fades away in favor of the play of sounds. Translation notes in some English Bibles try to explain the connections between objects and their significance, and *The Message* translation abandons the Hebrew names of the cities altogether, with Lachish becoming "Chariotville" and Adullam becoming "Glorytown." But the very fact that these puns do *not* translate well into English underscores the truth that the logical message of the passage is far from clear.

The view that ancient prophets were clear advocates for social justice assumes that the prophetic message was intended to be coherent. It assumes that metaphor, allusion, alliteration, and other poetic features were the means to an end: a message that, once deciphered, can be explicated in discursive, even homiletical style. The recognition of the highly complex literary style of the prophetic literature challenges this assumption. This poetry constructs a metaphor only to subvert it, turn it on its head, disassemble its pieces, and make something new. Every time we think we know what it means, it changes. By the time I had worked through Nahum carefully enough to write a commentary

(O'Brien 2002), for example, I felt battered by the attempt to make sense of it—the constantly shifting pronouns, the phrases that rhymed but remained babble, the rapid-fire images with no syntax. Trying to discern coherence in this book left me sympathetic with its opponent Nineveh, both of us victims of Nahum's brutal language.

In prophetic poetry, the metaphoric center doesn't hold. Rather than using language as rhetoric to move audiences to change their behaviors, prophetic poetry is *affective* rather than effective—designed to evoke feelings such as disgust, confusion, anger, or comfort rather than to offer a clear social platform. It "enlivens rather than enlightens" (Morris 1996, 74). The significance of this affective dimension of prophetic language is explored further in chapter 6.

WHOSE JUSTICE?

Over the past fifty years, professional biblical scholarship has undergone significant demographic changes. The voices of women, Asian Americans and African Americans, LGBTQ folk, persons from the Two-Thirds World, and differently abled interpreters are more (though still inadequately) prominent in the academy, as persons from more varied social locations present papers at international professional conferences, publish biblical commentaries, and function as public scholars on websites and podcasts. These newly recognized perspectives have challenged many of the dominant interpretations of biblical material, including the progressive claim that the prophets were pure advocates of justice for the marginalized. They have passionately shown that prophetic literature perpetuates injustice even as its rhetoric demands justice.

Feminist, Womanist, and Queer Perspectives

Since the 1970s, feminist interpreters have insisted that the prophetic books not only fail to advocate justice for women but actually harm women. Targeted for particular scorn has been the prophetic "marriage metaphor," the comparison of YHWH's relationship to Israel/Judah to that between a husband and wife. This comparison runs throughout the prophetic books—explicitly in Isaiah, Jeremiah, and Ezekiel, and perhaps implicitly in other books such as Malachi. But it is most clear in Hosea, which compares the relationship YHWH has with Israel to the relationship between the prophet and his wife Gomer.

While it had been traditional—and still is—to side with Hosea in this tale, to see him as a wronged man who graciously forgives his errant wife, feminists have pointed out the violence at the heart of this marriage. In Hosea 2, the husband threatens the wife with stripping, starvation, isolation, and death (2:3,

6, 10–13) and announces that he will have no pity on the children (2:4). He accuses the woman of taking other lovers (2:5, 7, 13). In the "happy ending" of the chapter, he isolates her in the wilderness (2:14). According to Renita Weems, if this is love, it is a battered love (Weems 1995). Ezekiel 16 and 23 make the sexualized violence of the metaphor even more clear: not only are the nations of Israel and Judah portrayed in graphically sexual terms but their punishment also entails stripping and death; YHWH's anger will only cease after he has taken his vengeance on the females' bodies (Ezek. 16:42).

Feminists have argued that these images not only reflect hatred of ancient women but also negatively affect readers in the present. In identifying the male prophet with YHWH, the marriage metaphor reinforces masculine imagery for the divine and in turn grants divine sanction for human male control of women through physical violence. The pleasure with which the texts explicitly recount the sexualized subjugation of the sinful woman (especially in Ezek. 23) has led to comparisons with pornography. According to the catchy phrase of Athalya Brenner, this rhetoric is "pornoprophetic" (Brenner 1996).

Feminist critique of the Prophets goes far beyond the marriage metaphor, however. When the question posed is "How does prophetic language affect women?" the prophets become violators of justice rather than its champions. For example, the book of Amos is the darling of those who place economic and social justice at the heart of religious faith, and many have joined Martin Luther King Jr. in making Amos's cry for justice as their own: "Let justice roll down like water / and righteousness like an everflowing stream" (Amos 5:24). Yet Amos does not advocate justice for women. In the *Women's Bible Commentary*, Judith Sanderson claims that the description of Samaria's women as greedy, callous cows in Amos 4:1–3 unfairly scapegoats women for the nation's ills. Since women in all cultures make up a disproportionate percentage of the poor, she laments that "Amos specifically condemned wealthy women for oppressing the poor (4:1) but failed specifically to champion the women among the poor" (Sanderson 1992, 206). If in ancient Israel women neither owned nor controlled property, why do they bear sole responsibility for how their husbands disseminate wealth?

I explore more of the concerns that feminist interpreters bring to the Prophets in my 2008 book *Challenging Prophetic Metaphor* (O'Brien 2008). Looking at the prophetic descriptions of YHWH as (abusing) Husband, (authoritarian) Father, and Jerusalem as a (defenseless) daughter reveals just how gendered these books are and how gendered ongoing interpretation of them is. My study of the book of Micah draws similar conclusions (O'Brien 2015). While Micah bemoans that women and children are cast out from their homes (2:9), the book remains silent on the causes of women's oppression and their unequal status in their society. The dire plight of women is invoked to elicit the reader's

sympathy or outrage regarding the seizing of land rather than to spur action
on behalf of women. When Jerusalem is depicted as a woman in Micah 4, she
is in labor and is threatened with rape before YHWH rescues her.

The problematic nature of prophetic imagery is further underscored by
womanist interpretation, an approach that attends to the intersections of sexism and racism in texts and readers. Grounded in the lived experience of African American women, womanist interpretation reveals the multiple layers of
oppression in prophetic literature. Wil Gafney's commentary in the Wisdom
Biblical Commentary series, for example, views the book of Nahum through
womanist lenses, and what she sees appalls her. The public sexual humiliation
of Woman Nineveh in Nahum 3 becomes not only rape but is "spectacle lynch-
ing" (Gafney 2017, 63). In her study of the book of Isaiah, Valerie Bridgeman
names the womanist imperative as asking what the prophet's language means for
women, children, and foreigners. She, along with others, highlights the various
ways in which the book denigrates children and makes them more vulnerable.
This is especially evident in Isaiah 1, in which children are blamed for "making"
their father beat them repeatedly. Bridgeman's experience of the danger faced
by Black children in the modern United States prevents her from excusing prophetic descriptions of child abuse as "only metaphor" (Bridgeman 2016, 321).

When the real-life consequences of prophetic language are taken seriously,
prophetic metaphors matter. They promote hierarchical and violent patterns
of human society by making them models for divine behavior. Ethical readings of the Prophets call readers not to imitate the prophets but to resist them.
In the clear words of Gafney, "The God who rapes is no God to me" (Gafney
2017, 64).

Queer interpreters have offered additional, often contrary, perspectives on
the metaphors of the Prophets. Challenging the assumption of many feminist
scholars that gender is a stable category, those reading with a queer lens point
to the gender-bending of prophetic texts and their subversive potential for
modern readers. For example, while I critique the image of Daughter as a
threshing heifer in Micah 4:13 as an image of subordination and dehumani-
zation, Erin Runions argues that it challenges traditional gender ideologies
by depicting a "more aggressive kind of femininity" (Runions 2001, 158).
Stuart Macwilliam reads the marriage metaphor of Jeremiah as challenging
patriarchy, since it places the male audience into the metaphorical position of
being good wives (Macwilliam 2002). In her commentary on Jeremiah, Carolyn Sharp insists that queer, feminist, and other readers committed to challenging patriarchy and heteronormativity must also resist prophetic rhetoric
when necessary, including Jeremiah's use of sexual shaming in Jeremiah 29:23
(Sharp 2021, 223) and glee in the physical and sexual assault of Zedekiah
in 38:19: "We are free to decline the mocking view of this as emasculating

weakness" and choose to stand with Zedekiah in defiance of phallocentric violence (Sharp 2021, 424–25).

Disability Studies

The study of the Bible in light of disability studies is still relatively new, but alongside other forms of contemporary criticism, its emerging insights are challenging the typical ways in which progressives have touted the prophets as advocates for justice for all. Rather than issuing simplistic complaints or optimistic praise about the ways that the prophetic texts describe those differently abled, this theoretical framework investigates the complex ways in which different bodies fare in the Prophets.

Throughout the prophetic literature, impaired bodies represent failure and abjection. Rebecca Raphael, for example, demonstrates that the book of Jeremiah compares Judah not only to promiscuous women but also disabled men who do not see, hear, or walk smoothly (Jer. 5–6): neither of these variations from the normative male can represent the faithful attitude toward YHWH (Raphael 2011, 112). Sarah Melcher explains that in the Latter Prophets metaphors of impairment often are used to describe moral deficiency (as in Ezek. 12:1–16), and impairment is the result of YHWH's punishment (as in Zeph. 1:14–18) (Melcher 2007, 123–25). When YHWH redeems the people, they are not valued as differently abled persons; their afflictions disappear when their moral rectitude is restored.

Jeremy Schipper's analysis of the Suffering Servant of Second Isaiah in light of disability studies points to the ways that the disabled are marginalized not only by the biblical text but, more importantly, its interpreters. When Christians spiritualize the image in Isaiah 52–53 of the afflicted Servant whose appearance is marred or assume that the figure is only temporarily impaired, they deny the possibility that those who live with nonnormative bodies can be representatives of the Divine. Interpreters of Second Isaiah and other prophetic texts often treat their language about the "blind," "lame," and "deaf" as symbols of theological attitudes (or even the corporate Israel) without considering the possibility that real disabled people are in view. As in Victorian literature, they function as "melodramatic instruments of moral instruction for able-bodied characters and readers" (Schipper 2011, 2). Schipper's perspective instead treats the disabled servant as a person.

Postcolonial Perspectives

Postcolonial criticism, which emerged in biblical scholarship in the 1990s, devotes close attention to the ways that texts and readers negotiate forces of political and cultural domination. It asks how biblical authors responded to the empires under whose domination they lived and worked—the Assyrians, the Babylonians, and the Persians—and how interpretations of the Bible are always political, even (and perhaps especially) when they are presented as the result of objective study. Postcolonial criticism has a strong historical component, seeking the details of how various empires and cultures manifested their power, but fundamentally it is a position of advocacy for the subjugated. In the words of Jeremiah Cataldo, "Postcolonialism is not passive. It is frustrated, if not irate. It demands justice, which it sees in the destruction of responsible oppressive institutional systems and powers" (Cataldo 2021, 342).

Postcolonial criticism also calls attention to how frequently Western interpreters describe the Prophets in theological rather than political terms, downplaying the social and cultural implications of their claims. Cataldo argues instead that the "restoration" of the community that the prophets seek was social and political, not merely "religious." Prophetic appeals to hope for the future and confidence in the ultimate power of Yahweh are closely tied to aspirations of some measure of local control of key institutions. In these images of restoration, however, hierarchies remain; within the community, priests wield power over others and returnees from Babylon are privileged over those labeled the "people of the land." Such dimensions in Isaiah's images of the future are explored further in chapter 7.

Repeatedly, prophets enforce boundaries between the community and others, often in ways overlooked by progressive interpreters. The complaint in Hosea 12:7 that traders "love to oppress" is often seen as advocacy for the poor, but Cataldo explains that the word for "traders" is closely related to the word for "Canaanite." The passage, he insists, is more of an attempt to control others by calling them Canaanites than an appeal to protect the vulnerable. By separating religion from politics, Cataldo claims, interpreters have colonized prophetic texts; by making the prophets forthtellers of universal ethics, interpreters have accepted the Prophets as their own rather than hear the distinctive politically charged voice of the ancient author (Cataldo 2021, 347).

The Militarization of the Prophets

The "prophets as social activists" orthodoxy tends to focus on what the prophets accuse the people of doing wrong. The blame that the prophets place on the community's wrongdoing is seen as an expression of their positive, proto-progressive values, the advocacy for those who have been wronged. These interpretations pay less attention to *what punishment* the prophets foretell: the destruction of the nation(s) in war.

Almost to a book, the Prophets proclaim that YHWH uses war to punish people. Running throughout books attributed to prophets living prior to the Babylonian destruction is the insistence that both Israel and Judah would be defeated in war because of the people's sins. Common, too, is the claim that YHWH punishes other nations through war. Nahum calls for the devastation of Nineveh. Isaiah insists that YHWH will use the Assyrians as the "rod of my anger" to punish unjust Judah (Isa. 10:5). And Jeremiah repeatedly explains that the Babylonian destruction of Judah is YHWH's doing:

> It is I who by my great power and my outstretched arm have made the earth, with the people and animals that are on the earth, and I give it to whomever I please. Now I have given all these lands into the hand of King Nebuchadnezzar of Babylon. (Jer. 27:5–6)

Isaiah 63 depicts YHWH as a blood-splattered warrior, robes stained red from trampling people in fury:

> Their juice spattered on my garments,
>   and stained all my robes. . . .
> I trampled down peoples in my anger,
>   I crushed them in my wrath,
>   and I poured out their lifeblood on the earth.
>   Isa. 63:3–6

This motif of YHWH the divine warrior who comes to wreak vengeance runs throughout the Prophets, right up into the closing chapters of Zechariah.

Not everyone is disturbed by this depiction of YHWH as a warrior or God using war for divine purposes. The predominately German-dominated scholarship of the World War I era actually praised the prophetic understanding of war. Intertwining his nationalist sentiments with his scholarship, Hermann Gunkel, a famous biblical scholar, wrote in 1916, in the midst of the war:

> The Old Testament gives a picture of a heroic nation; and so may we also, for whom war becomes the solution of the day, reach for this book. Our nation also remains invincible, if it knows both: the heroism of the sword and the heroism of faith. (qtd. in Washington 1997, 339)

Increasingly after World War II, however, many biblical scholars began to talk differently about the "heroism" of war. Gerhard von Rad, who was pressed into German military service in 1944 and suffered as a prisoner of war, claimed that holy war in Israel was purely defensive and when kings used the tradition of holy war for offense, the prophets turned the traditions against the monarchy (qtd. in Washington 1997, 340). In the decades that followed, the horror of the Nazi death camps became more widely known, due to the widespread dissemination in the 1970s of photos from the camps, the incorporation of Holocaust studies into university and college curriculums in the 1980s and 1990s, the opening of the Holocaust Memorial Museum in Washington in 1993, and the easy availability of Holocaust images on the internet by the 2000s; in turn, many later biblical scholars not only stressed the importance of combating anti-Semitism but also increasingly sought to explain or resist prophetic images of war.

This concern with the militarized violence of the Prophets has only multiplied over the past few decades, as examples of the brutality and illogic of war multiply. With increased media dissemination of images of wartime atrocities, greater exposure of the political and economic motivations for particular invasions, and a growing recognition of the physical and psychological trauma that war inflicts on combatants as well as victims, it is difficult to concur with the early-twentieth-century German scholar Otto Eissfeldt that in war "virtues shine forth" (qtd. in Washington 1997, 338). The plight of civilians fleeing armed conflict in Syria and around the world raises questions of how the prophetic foretelling or forthtelling of YHWH's pending acts of violence serves the marginalized. As David Clines notes, when Amos announces punishment on Israel for mistreating the poor, the means of that punishment—war—will oppress not only the rich but perhaps most especially those with the least resources (see Clines 1995, 91).

CONCLUSION

While the general statements in the prophetic literature about justice are inspiring, in this chapter I've tried to underscore that careful attention to the details of prophetic language complicates the categorical claim that the prophets were forthtellers of a clear message of social justice. The impressionistic, often cryptic, style of prophetic poetry makes it difficult to know what the words on their pages actually mean, and when diverse readers encounter the details of prophetic claims they do not always find advocacy for the marginalized. As philosophers and theologians have insisted, not everyone agrees about what justice actually entails. Whose wellbeing does "justice" assure? When the Prophets are read by those who prioritize the thriving of women, gender minorities, children, colonized societies, and victims of war, "Justice is turned back, and deliverance stands at a distance" (Isa. 59:14).

The historical dimensions of prophetic literature that I engaged in the previous chapter and the perspective of readers that I treated here both suggest just how shaky the progressive orthodoxy about the biblical prophets actually is. While much in the prophetic books does inspire hope, this material perpetuates many of the very ideologies that progressives so vehemently protest: racism, sexism, imperialism, ableism, and militarism. Maintaining this paradigm requires selective reading, the universalizing and generalizing of prophetic discourse, and denial of the ways in which the language of the prophetic books perpetuates problematic ideologies.

In the chapters that follow, I seek to explain the origins of this orthodoxy and how it became such common knowledge. If the prophets are not transparently advocates for social justice, how did this characterization come to dominate progressive thinking?

3

The Origins of a Progressive Orthodoxy

If the prophetic texts don't clearly present the prophets as social activists, then why do so many progressives think they do? Where did this interpretation come from? How did it become common knowledge? Researching this question takes us far beyond the Bible itself into the history of thinkers and scholars, into archives and personal correspondence. It demonstrates the power of not just ideas but the real-life human interactions that disseminate and popularize particular interpretations of the Bible.

This chapter has two goals—an informational one, to engage in contact tracing of the orthodoxy that the Israelite prophets were social activists, and an attitudinal one, to insist that to understand the Bible we must also understand the people who interpret the Bible and the way in which earlier generations of interpreters have shaped us, even (perhaps especially) when we are unaware of their influence. (For a more detailed description of this argument, see O'Brien 2022.)

BEFORE THE ENLIGHTENMENT

In early Christianity, including the New Testament, the conviction that the whole of the Jewish Scriptures but especially the Prophets had predicted the coming of Jesus was central to Christian teaching. We can see this conviction expressed throughout the Gospels (Luke 4; Matt. 1–2, 27); in key speeches in Acts (Acts 1; 8); and in Paul's letters (Rom. 11; 15). While using previous texts to support one's own views is often criticized as prooftexting, this interpretive strategy was quite common in the time period of these writers. Among the Dead Sea Scrolls are numerous examples of the *pesher*, the explication of how ancient prophetic texts actually refer to the interpreter's current day. According to *Pesher Habakkuk*, for example, God had given words to the prophet Habakkuk without revealing in what period they would be fulfilled. The Qumran community insisted that the biblical prophets were inspired by the Holy Spirit, but it also insisted that its leaders were able to discern the truth of the prophets' words more clearly than the prophets themselves.

In the subsequent centuries, additional interpretations of the Prophets developed among Christians. Martin Luther and John Calvin, for example, depicted the Hebrew prophets as preaching the law of Moses, in keeping with the Reformation insistence on the authority of Scripture. In his commentary on 1 Corinthians 14:3, for example, Calvin explained that "by the term prophecy, however, I do not understand the gift of foretelling the future, but as . . . the science of interpreting Scripture, so that a prophet is an interpreter of the will of God" (Calvin and Haroutunian 1958). The Reformers, however, did not abandon the historic Christian affirmation that the Old Testament prophets had foretold the life, death, and resurrection of Jesus. Instead, they promoted the idea of a dual role of prophecy: prediction *and* interpretation of the Word. This dual description persisted in later generations and was included in *Webster's English Dictionary* in 1828.

THE ENLIGHTENMENT AND
SCIENTIFIC BIBLICAL CRITICISM

The first real challenge to the predictive approach to prophecy was an epistemological one. In the seventeenth, eighteenth, and nineteenth centuries, rationalists, Deists, and skeptics (mostly in Europe and Great Britain) insisted that knowledge is not granted by supernatural means but by the careful application of human reason. Believing that truth should be self-evident to all rational *men* (italics intentional), Enlightenment thinkers sought rational rather than supernatural explanations of miracles and of the prophets' reception of knowledge. The Dutch philosopher and scientist Baruch Spinoza posited natural explanations for biblical accounts of miracles and prophetic inspiration, and the English philosopher David Hume denied the possibility of both supernatural prophecy and miracles on the basis that both are beyond verification by human observation and reason. If Christianity was to have any value for reasonable people, Hume argued, it would need to be understood as a set of natural and universal moral values, not a set of historical events revealed in advance to the prophets of the Old Testament. Counterattacks to these "new" ideas about prophecy ensued, voiced by traditionalist Christians committed to predictive interpretations of the prophet, including Sir Isaac Newton, who insisted that the fulfillment of prophecy is the foundation of Christianity (Force 1982). Yet the rationalist characterization of prophets as bold speakers of truth grew in popularity among intellectuals throughout the seventeenth and eighteenth centuries. Increasingly, prophets were described not as faithful exhorters of Scripture but rather as those who spoke out against outmoded traditional thought. Already by 1647, the English clergyperson Jeremy Taylor equated the verb "prophesy" with speaking on the basis of one's conscience (Taylor 1647).

A key development in the progressive understanding of the Prophets can be attributed to the English scholar Robert Lowth, who in a series of lectures in 1753 argued that the speech of the Hebrew prophets was not articulate discourse but instead obscure poetry borne of inspiration: the "spontaneous overflow from the heart of an artist moved by passion" (Henderson 2019, 132). The link between prophecy and poetry was developed further by Romantic poets such as William Blake, Samuel Taylor Coleridge, and William Wordsworth, who cast the ancient prophets as "poetic geniuses" and suggested the prophetic nature of their own poetry.

The fusion of rationalist and Romantic views of prophecy was endowed with weighty academic credentials in late-eighteenth- and nineteenth-century Germany. At prominent German universities such as that at Göttingen, founded in 1737 as an "Enlightenment" institution, an influential chain of professors whose students in turn joined the faculty devoted themselves to the retrieval of the *true* history of ancient Israel. (Paul Kurtz estimates that, during this period, between one-half and one-third of professors at universities were related by blood or educational training [Kurtz 2018, 26].) Declaring themselves not bound to the Bible's own description of events or the teachings of the church, they distinguished between what *actually* happened in ancient Israel and what prescientific people in biblical times *thought* had happened. In the words of Thomas Howard, study of the Bible turned from its theology to its origins (Howard 2000). Biblical texts became less the basis for belief than a dataset from which the past could be rationally and systematically reconstructed. And in this reconfiguration of biblical studies into a scientific discipline, the prophets were granted moral and, eventually, chronological superiority.

Johann Eichhorn, who joined the Göttingen faculty in 1788 after studying under the historian J. D. Michaelis and encountering Lowth's views on poetry through the work of the philosopher and historian Johann Herder, offered rational explanations for predictions of the future and miracles and described the prophets as public leaders. His student Heinrich Ewald—who succeeded him on the Göttingen faculty in 1827 and was dismissed twice from the university for his political stances (once as part of the Göttingen Seven that included the Brothers Grimm)—was an advocate for an unfettered pursuit of history.

Ewald also was enamored of the prophets, whom he portrayed as so attuned to the "pure Source of all Energy" that they perceived present, past, and future. According to Ewald, the prophets insisted upon the worship of YHWH alone and the ethical treatment of others, promoting ethics over against the rituals of the Israelite cult and Canaanite polytheism (Henderson 2019).

Julius Wellhausen, Ewald's most famous student, joined the Göttingen faculty in 1882. He is best known for his study of the Pentateuch and his advancement of the Documentary Hypothesis, which does not credit the first five books of the Bible to Moses but casts them as four later anonymous documents composed over the long span of Israelite history: the first, J, during the time of the Israelite monarchy and the last, P, by priests in the postexilic period, when the survivors of the exile returned to the land of Judah and reestablished the Temple under the auspices of the Persian Empire. Less discussed but foundational to his reconstruction of the Pentateuch are Wellhausen's claims about prophecy. He insisted that the prophets, living long before the composition of the Pentateuch, heard God speaking to them directly, apart from any religious tradition. But in the postexilic period, he complained, Israelite priests imposed the deadly Priestly source on earlier material, smothering the original vitality of Israelite faith with the weight of the Law and turning it into a theocratic "Judaism": "If the Priestly Code makes the cultus the principal thing, that appears to amount to a systematic decline into the heathenism which the prophets incessantly combated and yet were unable to eradicate" (Wellhausen [1881] 1983, 423). By dating the prophets prior to the Pentateuch, Wellhausen made them quite literally the origin of Israelite faith. In his influential 1881 article "Israel" in the ninth edition of the *Encyclopedia Britannica*, he added to this portrait a characterization that would soon become ubiquitous: the prophets were the founders of "ethical monotheism." Wellhausen had adopted this phrase from another scholar, the Dutch liberal Abraham Kuenen, who maintained that the prophets created this philosophical and ethical concept: according to Kuenen, it was the "better thing [that] was produced by Israelitisch prophecy, and completed by Jesus, the greatest of the prophets" (Muir 1877, xxxvii).

By the end of the nineteenth century, German scholars had crafted a clear and, for many, compelling portrait of the prophets. No longer predicters of the future, prophets were inspired and inspiring individuals who advanced ethics. Indeed, such became the very definition of "prophet" in the work of Wilhelm Gesenius, another student of Eichhorn trained at Göttingen. Gesenius's lexica of Hebrew and Greek, based on "scientific" principles and bolstered with comparative linguistics, went through scores of editions and were translated into multiple languages. The 1827 English translation of his Hebrew lexicon by U.S. scholar Josiah Gibbs (repeated in the 1828 and 1832 editions), explained that the Hebrew verb "to prophesy" means "to bring forth, to shew, to announce," such that the primary meaning of the verb is "to speak as God's ambassador." By 1850 the Greek-English lexicon by U.S. scholar Edward Robinson cited Gesenius's study of Hebrew to suggest that the Greek equivalent *prophetes* means "to pour forth words of divine inspiration" rather than to predict the future.

This portrait was presented not as a confessional creed but the results of the scientific, unfettered pursuit of history. And yet evident in the work of these historians is the strong legacy of Romanticism. Not only the Romantic poets such as Wordsworth, Blake, and Coleridge but also these German biblical scholars valued the primitive origins of religion as the fount of creativity and inspiration, finding in the past heroic individuals whose individual experience and closeness to the natural world granted them vitality, authenticity, and spiritual authority.

Also running through the work of German scholars was the strong influence of Lutheran theology, particularly its strong demarcation between law and grace. According to Luther, the law of the Old Testament only served to reveal human sinfulness, while humans' salvation from their disordered selves is dependent solely on faith in Jesus/God and not on the performance of any rituals or "works." Luther insisted that the biblical prophets advanced precisely this doctrine: they "instructed the church in the true nature of faith, justification by faith alone, and the proper distinctions between Law and Gospel" (Pak 2018, 109). Despite Wellhausen's protestations that he was a historian and not a theologian, through his use of history he was able to denigrate law (for Wellhausen, the Torah riddled with the ritualism of the Priestly source) and prioritize grace (for Wellhausen, the free individual expressions of the prophets). German scholars insisted that the prophets had preached ethics from the beginning, such that deviations from this pure religion were impositions on the truth, errors perpetuated in Judaism. Only with the teaching of Jesus—and in the reformation of Martin Luther—was religion restored to its pure prophetic origins.

THE POPULARIZATION OF GERMAN SCHOLARSHIP

Throughout the nineteenth century, German scholarship was increasingly translated into English and popularized throughout Great Britain and the United States, touted as scientific evidence that prophets were not predicters of the future. A key figure in this popularization was the British interpreter W. Robertson Smith, the first major English-speaking scholar to incorporate German scholarship. He not only lectured widely about Ewald, Duhm, and Wellhausen at the University of Cambridge and in public venues but also promoted their publications. He penned the introduction to the 1885 English translation of Wellhausen's master work, the *Prolegomena*, and hired Wellhausen to write that influential article on Israel in the ninth edition of the *Encyclopedia Britannica*; this contribution popularized his historical sketch of ancient Israel and the idea that the prophets were the founders of ethical monotheism and promoters of religious individualism. Smith's own 1882 volume, *The Prophets of Israel*, in which he states his goal as popularizing biblical science and extending the insights of Ewald, Duhm, and "my friend Professor Wellhausen," interpreted the preexilic prophets in their own historical contexts and characterized them as teaching a "heart that delights in acts of piety and loving-kindness" (Smith 1882, 372).

By midcentury, a clever catchphrase accompanied this interpretation of prophecy. In an 1852 magazine, the Scottish Unitarian clergyman William Maccall described the prophet as "forthteller" and not a "foreteller"—a speaker of truth rather than a predicter. In this article in other publications, he ridiculed those who believe in supernatural sources of knowledge and praised heroic individuals who defy establishment thinking. Within fifty years, the "forthteller not foreteller" descriptor of the prophet had become ubiquitous, cited in sermons, lectures, textbooks, popular books, and, perhaps most importantly, in reference volumes, including *Strong's Concordance* (Strong 1890) the *Cambridge Greek Testament for Schools and Colleges* (Lias 1892), and the *Sermon Bible* (Nicoll 1900, 221). In these academic resources, various German scholars and especially Gesenius's lexical volumes were repeatedly cited as objective verification that prophecy did not involve prediction.

Although the transformation of the prophet from foreteller to forthteller was accomplished by the end of the nineteenth century, the prophets had not yet become true social critics. They had become anti-institutional but not yet interested in the transformation of the structures of society. They were forthtellers of individual faith rather than of systemic change. To witness that further transformation of the prophetic message, we turn our attention to the United States in the early twentieth century.

PROPHETS BECOME SOCIAL CRITICS

In the early twentieth century, mainline theological schools in Great Britain and the United States touted German biblical scholarship as the benchmark for scientific study of the Bible. At Lancaster Theological Seminary (founded in 1825 by the German Reformed Church in the United States), Professor Frederick Gast promulgated German scholarship through publications in the *Reformed Church Review* and through his teaching of Reformed clergy. Archived copies of student lecture notes from Old Testament introductory courses record that he systematically walked students through the arguments of Ewald, Wellhausen, and Wilhelm de Wette (another famous German scholar who had helped raise funds for the founding of the seminary for the purposes of extending German scholarship in North America) (deWette 1826). As commemorated in a plaque now located in the rear of the seminary chapel, Gast's title was changed from Professor of Old Testament Theology to Professor of Hebrew and Old Testament *Science* in 1904.

German scientific biblical scholarship was also disseminated through a network of scholars at Union Theological Seminary in New York City. Charles Briggs, a Presbyterian scholar who graduated from Union in 1863, studied with Ewald before joining the Union faculty in 1874. In 1892 his major address at Union, "The Authority of Holy Scripture," grounded in German scholarship, prompted charges of heresy from the Presbyterian Church, and the heresy trial helped popularize Wellhausen's ideas in the United States. Francis Brown, Briggs's student at Union (known to many students of Hebrew through his contributions to the Brown-Driver-Briggs lexicon), joined the Union faculty in 1879.

Instead of simply being replicated, however, German scholarship was also being transformed through its appropriation in the United States in the early twentieth century, most strikingly in the Social Gospel movement. Advocates of the Social Gospel insisted that Christianity is not only concerned with people's souls but even more importantly with the actual physical conditions of their lives; they framed poverty, poor labor conditions, war, and other social ills as religious problems, and they articulated the message of Christianity so as to address the problems facing the world. Embracing the intellectual and theological framework of modernism, the Social Gospel movement extolled scientific progress and the potential of humans to improve the world's material conditions. Bolstered by science, society could shed the shackles of the past and inaugurate a more hopeful future. German biblical scholarship, for the Social Gospel, became one of the many branches of the sciences, all of which rely on reason rather than superstition and outline the path of human progress.

Throughout the literature of the Social Gospel, scientific biblical scholarship on the prophets was turned into an appeal for social transformation. Every address recorded in the 1907 Minutes of the National Council of Congregational Churches of the United States (including that of outgoing moderator Washington Gladden, often considered the vanguard of the Social Gospel) appealed to reason and critical biblical scholarship to bolster the call to addressing social ills: given new understandings of science, modern men know that miracles do not really happen and that predictions of the future are not possible (National Council of Congregational Churches, 1907). In a later volume articulating the "social ministry," Detroit pastor George Elliott cited W. Robertson Smith to affirm that prophets are "forthtellers rather than fore-tellers," "practical politicians and social reformers" (Elliott 1910, 15). In his 1913 publication *Christianity and the Social Crisis*, Baptist Walter Rauschenbusch insisted that the prophets were ethical reformers of unjust economic policies and proto-Christians:

> Jesus clasped hands with the entire succession of the prophets with whom he classed John. Their words were his favorite quotations. Like them he disregarded or opposed the ceremonial elements of religion and insisted on the ethical. Like them he sided with the poor and oppressed. (Rauschenbusch 1907, 53)

In Harry Emerson Fosdick, perhaps the most popular face of the Social Gospel movement, scientific biblical scholarship and modernism were fully fused with the characterization of the prophet as a social activist. Fosdick, who joined the Union faculty after studying under Brown, popularized the view that prophets are social critics. In his popular publications such as *Guide to Understanding the Bible* and the aptly named *Modern Use of the Bible*, he alluded to German scholarship on the actual dating of biblical books and relied on reason when encountering biblical comments about demons. Without going into detail on the sources of the Pentateuch, he asserted that the Law was "still plastic and uncanonical" before the exile (Fosdick 1938, 224), and throughout his works he described the prophets as promoting ethical monotheism and opposition to the law, the clearest precursor to Jesus. But while the German Wellhausen had resisted political interpretations of the prophets, complaining that his teacher Ewald was too political, Fosdick used the results of higher criticism to demonstrate that what the prophets forthtold was a message of social change. He insisted,

> What [the prophets] had tried to do in their times and fashion [Jesus] tried to do in his—take monotheism morally in earnest . . . . demand-ing not ritualistic conformity but moral genuineness within and broth-erly conduct without. . . . So truly was Jesus as a Hebrew prophet in the great succession from Amos and Hosea on, that from the begin-ning a powerful social conscience was injected into Christianity. (Fos-dick 1938, 40, 80)

As his archives at Union Theological Seminary reveal, Fosdick taught such views in seminary courses on the prophets and before large crowds at Riverside Church in New York City, where he pastored. He also contributed prolifically to publications including the *Atlantic Monthly*, *Good Housekeeping*, the *Christian Century*, and *Ladies' Home Journal*. He published over sixty times

in the *Reader's Digest*. One of the highest-profile preachers of the early twentieth century and an early master of media, he also conducted regular radio
programs and graced the cover of *Time* magazine in 1930. In all of these
venues, he invoked the prophets and the prophetic Jesus as teachers of social
reform.

Wellhausen and especially Gunkel had individualized the prophets, imag-
ining their biographies and their distinctive personalities. In a similar vein,
Fosdick helped readers picture courageous individual prophets standing up
to unjust institutions. He frequently "reconstructed" the actual scenarios in
which Isaiah issued his words (Fosdick 1938, 63), and at Union he regularly
taught the course "Exposition of Jeremiah," that prophet with "the richest
experience of personal religion . . . known on earth before our Lord" (Miller
1985, 320), helping cement Jeremiah's status as the paradigm of the tortured,
lonely prophetic individual opposed to injustice.

Not surprisingly, Fosdick and the key architects of the Social Gospel movement were not Lutherans but Calvinists. Far more optimistic than Lutherans about the ability for society to improve, the followers of John Calvin
sought social reform. Just as Calvin used biblical law to organize Geneva as
a Christian city and the Puritans of New England made Old Testament law
the basis of the Massachusetts Bay Colony, so too Gladden (Congregational-
ist), Rauschenbusch (Baptist), and Fosdick (Baptist) sought to make the world
a more godly place. Their formation in Calvinist churches and educational
institutions was instrumental in their embrace of scientific modernism as a
tool of reform.

In Fosdick and the Social Gospel, the prophet remained a courageous
individual hero who stands alone, often at great personal peril, but the prophet's opposition was now directed against unjust social institutions. While the
Lutheran Wellhausen eschewed politics in his own life and in his portrait of
ancient Israel, the Calvinist Fosdick made the prophets political and socially
concerned. The portrait of the prophet once forged in the fusion of intellectual and theological trends in Lutheran Germany became the scientific basis
for a very Calvinist movement.

FURTHER SPREAD

From these roots in the Social Gospel, the equation of the "prophetic" with
social justice spread throughout progressive Christianity in the twentieth
century. It is reflected, for example, in the primary manifesto of Liberation
Theology, Gustavo Gutiérrez's 1971 *Teología de la liberación*. A Peruvian working within the Dominican order, Gutiérrez spurred the Church to adopt a

"preferential option for the poor" based on the precedent of the Hebrew prophets. He quoted various biblical scholars to insist that prophets do not predict the future but point the way to economic justice (Gutiérrez 1988, 10, 69). While firmly situated in Latin America, Gutiérrez had studied in Europe—philosophy at the University of Louvain and theology at the Faculty of Theology in Lyons, France—where he encountered now standard academic views of the prophets and transformed them to a call for social protest.

A similar use of the term "prophetic" pervades the inaugural publication of the Black Liberation Theology movement: James Cone's *A Black Theology of Liberation* ([1970] 2010). In this important volume, Cone demanded liberation from the racism permeating Christianity and found biblical precedent in three key biblical moments: the exodus event, the teaching of Jesus, and the Hebrew prophets. "The consistent theme in Israelite prophecy is Yahweh's concern for the lack of social, economic, and political justice for those who are poor and unwanted in society. . . . The prophets of Israel are prophets of social justice" (Cone [1970] 2010, 19). Cone's depiction of the prophets both depended on yet extended beyond its predecessors in German scholarship and the Social Gospel: with Wellhausen and Fosdick he concurred that, in the prophetic tradition, speech about God "will always move on the brink of treason and heresy in an oppressive society" (Cone [1970] 2010, 62), but he turned this critique against the very white traditions they represented and defined oppression as Black oppression.

In a less direct though highly influential way, the characterization of prophecy as forthtelling rather than foretelling also was promoted outside of theological circles within secular studies of religion. One pathway for its dissemination was the work of Max Weber, the German thinker whose work undergirded the creation of the modern discipline of sociology and its subdiscipline the sociology of religion. In his major publications—*The Protestant Ethic and the Spirit of Capitalism, Economy and Society,* and *Ancient Judaism,* Weber argued that religions develop from polytheism into monotheism and then ethical monotheism; religious innovation is sparked by charismatic figures but over time dies with the "routinization of charisma" into institutional bureaucracy. In the case of Judaism, he maintained, the polytheistic faith of the early tribes developed under the prophets into ethical monotheism, but the prophets' genius was choked in the postexilic period by hierocratic priests who resigned themselves to accepting the role of the Jewish community in the Persian Empire as a "pariah" community—a sect that abandoned hope of social transformation in this world and turned to apocalyptic expectations.

Weber consistently acknowledged that he drew his evidence from the work of other scholars. He sometimes explicitly named his sources for the study of ancient Israel (Wellhausen, Gunkel, and Eduard Meyer, who studied with

Ewald alongside Wellhausen); but in keeping with an era of scholarship less concerned with citation than today's, many of his sources remain uncited. His claims about prophecy, for example, seem to clearly rely on Wellhausen's historical sequencing of the sources underlying the Old Testament, and he shares with scholars from Michaelis through Wellhausen the denigration of the postexilic period. In Weber's scheme, as in Wellhausen's and Wellhausen's predecessors Michaelis and Herder, a once-vibrant Israelite faith declined into an isolated, priestly controlled Judaism. Weber employed German biblical scholarship differently than did the Social Gospel movement, insisting that neither the prophets nor Jesus were social reformers (Weber [1968] 1978, 444), and yet his description of the "routinization of charisma," the strong dichotomy he drew between charismatic prophets and bureaucratized priests, and the "pariah" label he placed on the postexilic Jewish community advanced even further the view of prophets as chronological prior to and ethically superior to law-bound priests. In an argument that sounds astonishingly more Protestant than secular, Weber relied heavily on Wellhausen's reconstruction to advance his argument that

> [Prophecy] vanished because the priestly police power in the Jewish congregation gained control over ecstatic prophecy in the same manner as did the bishopric and Presbyterian authorities over pneumatic prophecy in the early Christian congregation. (Weber 1952, 380)

It is a great irony, then, that during the twentieth century many departments of religion or theology were renamed departments of religious studies, and scholars abandoned research methodologies grounded in confessional categories for seemingly more objective approaches such as Weber's.

CONCLUSION

My goal in tracing the origins of the progressive orthodoxy about prophets is not to challenge the value of progressive convictions. As I explore further in the next chapter, the characterization of the prophets as voices for social justice has much to commend it. The scholarship from which it draws has been instrumental in drawing critical attention to previously neglected dimensions of biblical texts, and for over a hundred years it has fueled action on behalf of the marginalized. This orthodoxy about the prophets is not completely *wrong* or *bad*.

But I have sought to demonstrate that equating the prophet with the social activist is not an objective, "plain sense" interpretation of prophetic texts. It is instead an interpretation crafted over time, within particular historical and theological contexts by particular people. In the words of Paul Kurtz, "Any academic orthodoxy did not arise from nowhere" (Kurtz 2016, 585). The origins of this orthodoxy can be traced through the Enlightenment, Romanticism, nineteenth-century German biblical scholarship, and the Social Gospel, and the success of its popularization can be credited not only to Liberation Theology movements but also, ironically, to particular frameworks for the sociology of religion. This interpretation emerged at a particular time and place not because it is more accurate than other interpretations but because it resonated with and bolstered particular interests and convictions. Its ideological underpinnings serve similar functions today.

The chapter that follows reflects on the legacy of this orthodoxy. What have been its contributions and its dangers? Why does the way we talk about prophecy matter?

4

Evaluating an Orthodoxy

My discussion so far has stressed two main ideas. In chapters 1 and 2 I explained the many legitimate ways to understand prophecy in the Hebrew Bible; prophets are not always unabashed champions of social justice. In chapter 3 I traced the networks by which progressive Protestantism and secular culture became convinced that prophets are "forthtellers not foretellers," raising their voices not to predict the future but to instigate social change. Although shaped in part by earlier Enlightenment rationalist thought, the orthodoxy was given the weight of "science" by nineteenth-century German biblical scholars and wedded to social justice causes in the twentieth century. There is a reason why "prophetic preaching" in a liberal religious context means something quite specific.

In this chapter I offer some evaluation of the implications of this orthodoxy. What good work has it accomplished, and what harm has it done? Who has benefited from its construction? Who has not?

LIBERAL AND ROMANTIC INDIVIDUALISM

Throughout this progressive orthodoxy, the Hebrew prophets are depicted as men of fierce individualist ethics: they lambasted corrupt leaders, resisted idolatry, and opposed ritual, religious tradition, and the priesthood that maintained these traditions. Clearly evident in this characterization is the imprint of the Enlightenment belief in the primacy of the individual. Long before the Göttingen pipeline was laid, John Locke and others had built philosophical, political, and educational systems grounded in a belief in the inalienable rights of individuals, each of whom should be able to enjoy the freedom of conscience. Also evident in this view of the prophetic individual is Romanticism's

54

emotionalism, in which the inspired and lonely outsider who invites our empathy and compassion becomes the ultimate hero.

Wellhausen built upon these foundations when he exalted individual faith over organized religion. He actually considered the Hebrew prophets' attempts to make morality the basis of a nation a mistake (Wellhausen [1881] 1973, 491) and praised Jeremiah for proclaiming that the law would be put upon the heart (Jer. 31:33) instead of the nation (Wellhausen [1881] 1973, 491). Gunkel and Weber likewise located the impetus for change in charismatic individuals who work outside of institutions. Fosdick stated it plainly in his lecture aptly titled "Plea for Genuine Individualism": "Jesus certainly was an individualist. . . . Collective hope was rooted back in indefatigable care about the endless worth and possibility of the individual" (Fosdick 1933, 39); "Christianity tries to change men's souls in order to change their societies, and it tries to change their societies in order to give their souls a chance" (Fosdick 1936, 40). A strong attachment to the weeping, solitary prophet Jeremiah, not surprisingly, runs like an unbroken thread throughout the writings of Fosdick and Weber and into the present.

In the present, progressive traditions continue to define the "prophetic" as the work of individuals courageously standing up for truth. Rev. Dr. Martin Luther King Jr. and Rev. Dr. Jeremiah Wright are labeled as modern prophets, and homiletics dictionaries and textbooks define "prophetic preaching" as addressing social ills. In a secular context, an NPR music critic in 2017 deemed Kendrick Lamar's album *DAMN* "prophetic": "[Prophets] did not come to praise or worship, but to destroy and rebuild. With a sense of duty that compelled them to speak truth to power, they faced frequent persecution, imprisonment, even death. Prophets rarely won popularity contests, at least not without being beheaded for it later" (Carmichael 2017).

This individualist reading of the Prophets has functioned in many positive ways. It has emboldened individuals to stand up to injustice and garnered biblical support for those who do not blindly follow unscrupulous leaders. Yet individualism comes with costs.

In *After Whiteness,* Willie James Jennings lyrically and devastatingly unveils this idolatry of "white self-sufficient masculinity" in Western education and especially theological education (Jennings 2020). The "educated" person is "bound in courage, moral vision, and singularity of purpose" (Jennings 2020, 31); he manages himself, commands all knowledge, and ultimately seeks to control the world. Through their policies and practices, institutions endeavor to replicate the self-sufficient mastery of knowledge in which their faculty excel, "caught up in the historical trajectory of a plantation pedagogy that teaches us how to be institutional men, which is how to aim at becoming master" (Jennings 2020, 18). Learners are taught to admire and desire that

image of the one who masters his field. Not surprisingly, in educational institutions those who do not conform to this image are marginalized: those who
value collaborative forms of learning and those who demand attention to their
own embodiment. Jennings tells poignant stories, gathered while serving as the
dean of a mostly white university divinity school, of faculty and students of
color (and women) whose intelligence was denied because they failed to emu-
late these Enlightenment values.

   We also pay the cost of individualism when preachers lambast their congregations while defending their right to be "prophetic" and dismiss any resistance
to such screeds as yet another example of those in power silencing those who
point out wrong. Given the definition of the prophet as such an agitator, it
should not surprise us that textbooks and monographs caution preachers to
balance their "prophetic" role with their "pastoral" one (Tisdale 2010). But as
I've been arguing, we *should* be surprised by the ready assumption that opposition to one's community is the definition of "prophetic." If, as redaction critics
have argued, these texts are not the products of individuals but of generations
over time, perhaps we might reclaim the prophetic role of communities that
seek to understand God working in their midst. In chapter 8, I suggest the value
that comes from recognizing the communal nature of the book of Jeremiah.

CHRISTIANS AND JEWS

One really positive use of the "prophets as social activists" orthodoxy about
prophecy is in challenging anti-Jewish readings of the Christian Old Testament. Christians have a long, ugly history of supersessionism—the teaching
that, as punishment for their disobedience, God annulled all promises once
made to the Jewish people and made a new agreement (a new covenant, a
New Testament) in which all of the treasures of ancient Israel (and none of
the difficulties) would be inherited by those who believe in Jesus. A study of
church history makes it clear that predictive readings of the Prophets has gone
hand-in-hand with anti-Judaism. Throughout European Christian art, Isaiah
and Jeremiah are shown behind or underneath scenes of Jesus' infancy, holding up scrolls on which their predictions of Jesus are recorded; and sculpture
work on cathedral facades depicts the synagogue as a blindfolded, defeated
woman beside whom stands a triumphant and clear-eyed female church. The
same theology can be found in the words of Christian theologians such as
Cyril of Alexandria and Justin Martyr, who insisted that if Jews can't recognize that their own Scriptures reveal that Jesus is the Messiah, then they
must be willfully blind (Williamson 1982). Over the course of history, this dismissal of Judaism has explicitly and implicitly granted theological sanction to

actions and inactions that treat the Jewish people as disposable. In the past few decades, we have increasingly recognized the ways in which supersessionism fueled Nazi ideologies. The blame for Hitler's Final Solution cannot be laid solely at the feet of Christianity, but it is undeniable that centuries-long Christian anti-Jewish tropes helped Nazism "stick."

Taking responsibility for disrupting anti-Jewish biblical interpretation, biblical studies textbooks since the 1970s (especially those with a theological orientation) have taken an explicitly post-Holocaust perspective. Students are encouraged to not use the derogatory term "Old Testament" but instead the more neutral "Hebrew Bible." Authors challenge Christian supersessionism in their introductory pages and insist that the text should be interpreted on its own terms and alongside Jewish readers. They not only proclaim that prophets were "forthtellers not foretellers" but also model a way of reading that does not limit the meaning of the text to its Christian usage. For example, most argue at some length that when Isaiah 7 describes a child named Immanuel, it does not point to Jesus whose birth was still seven hundred years in the future but to an ancient child whose coming of age would correlate with a particular outcome in the war in which Jerusalem was waging in the eighth century BCE. In the historical and literary context of the book of Isaiah, the passage underscores God's intention to use the Assyrian armies to punish Judah's sins rather than to promise eternal salvation through a messiah. At its best, such interpretations challenge the charge that Jews have denied the "plain sense" of their own text and also invite Christian readers to recognize the way that people before the time of Jesus believed God was working with them. This, indeed, is the way that I interpret and teach the prophetic books.

For all its value, however, the "forthtellers, not foretellers" orthodoxy is not problem-free. The German science on which liberal orthodoxy was erected, overviewed in the previous chapter, was not Jewish-friendly. In the nineteenth century, the Lutheranism in which Herder, Eichhorn, Ewald, and Wellhausen were steeped was not simply a religion but also a national ethos, deeply ingrained in the country's psyche. By translating the Bible into the German vernacular, Luther had turned the Bible into a German text; as Jonathan Sheehan describes it, "the German Bible simultaneously created a German religion, a German culture, and a German nation"—it became a cultural Bible (Sheehan 2005, 227). And Luther's way of reading the Bible had become a cultural heritage as well. Read through Luther's eyes, the Bible promoted individual belief over ritual—and, in turn, privileged Protestants over others who erroneously valued ritual, especially Jews and Catholics.

By adopting Wellhausen's sequencing of sources in which P is a late perversion of Israel's prophetic faith, Christian interpreters could effectively dismiss Judaism in God's plan of salvation. They could credit the ethical impulse of true faith to the prophets rather than Israel's law or ongoing history. They could claim continuity with Israelite origins while denigrating the era leading up to Jesus; Jesus became the reclamation of a lost prophetic genius, the resurrection of prophecy long after it had died. While it would be unfair to blame Wellhausen and other nineteenth-century scholars for all the ways their ideas were used to support Nazism in the twentieth century, their ideas did help perpetuate and give "scientific" validity to later anti-Jewish and eventually anti-Semitic ideologies. Their success in making Christianity "Jew-free" benefited later attempts to make Germany Jew-free: they did not instigate anti-Jewish violence, but they advanced anti-Jewish thought that made the violence seem reasonable (Heschel 2008).

In a different way, the Calvinist underpinnings of the Social Gospel also allowed anti-Jewish thought to continue. Although Calvinist thought retained a place for the law in human improvement (unlike Lutheranism), its advocates also advanced anti-Jewish tropes. Giving the credit for ethics to the Israelite prophets (the precursors of the ultimate prophet, Jesus), rather than to the "moribund" law and "Jewish" ritual, speakers such as Fosdick perpetuated negative stereotypes of ancient Israelite religious faith (and Judaism itself) by divorcing the ritual from the ethical:

> How sharp the contrast is between [Jesus] and the popular religion of his day! To be sure, in the rabbis are insights and intuitions that are deep and beautiful. . . . While at times, however, we do discover these fine insights, how trivial were the preoccupations of popular religion in Jesus' day! (Fosdick 1924, 199)

These anti-Jewish tropes continue in the present, despite post-Holocaust attempts to reclaim the Jewishness of Jesus. Progressives tend to dismiss the sacrificial and purity systems outlined in Exodus, Leviticus, and Deuteronomy as superstitious ritual in favor of the prophetic commands to do justice. They rarely recognize that the very ethical values that progressives uphold are embedded in the Torah and in the practices of ancient and modern Judaism: care for the poor (Deut. 15:7–11), protections for the stranger and the worker (Exod. 22:20; Deut. 24:14), and loving one's neighbor as oneself (Lev. 19:17–18). While on the surface, lionizing the prophets seems to honor the Jewish Bible, this version of the prophets does something else: it lifts the prophets out of the Old Testament, making them an ethical core extractable from the ritual dross of the Jewish faith.

In turn, the insistence that the prophets must advocate for social justice encourages a highly selective reading of and hierarchy of value within the prophetic books themselves. Haggai's focus on the rebuilding of the Temple (Hag. 1), Malachi's concern with proper offerings (Mal. 1:6–14), Obadiah's call for vengeance against Edom (Obadiah), and Nahum's call for vengeance against Nineveh (Nahum) are denigrated as pseudoprophetic or a decline of prophecy—the beginning of Judaism rather than a valid dimension of Israelite prophecy. Anything in the Prophets that expounds otherworldly visions and pessimism about human progress is deemed "apocalyptic" rather than "classical prophecy." All that does not fit the progressive orthodoxy is excluded from the category of "prophet" so that the definition of prophet as a social critic can be preserved.

As I demonstrate in later chapters, the imposition of this orthodoxy on even the progressives' favorite prophets Amos and Jeremiah encourages interpreters to overlook aspects of what these books actually say. In my long career of teaching in religious settings, I have repeatedly witnessed the deep cognitive dissonance that occurs when readers are forced to read all of these books rather than selected passages—facing the stark contrast between their expectations of the prophets and the words recorded in this literature. The cognitive dissonance intensifies when they encounter the critique of the books' ideologies offered by interpreters of diverse social locations. How can these paragons of justice say *that*? In the Prophets as in relationships, accepting that those whom we have lauded as heroes do harm is incredibly difficult and painful.

The explicit and implicit anti-Judaism of extracting the prophets from the Jewish tradition also extends into interpretations of Jesus as a prophet who stood in opposition to the Jewish faith of his day. Pervasively in progressive discourse, Jesus is contrasted with other Jews, particularly Jewish leaders. They were exclusive while he was inclusive; they were nationalistic while he embraced all nations; they were rule-bound while he only followed the law of love; they were misogynist, patriarchal, and heteronormative while he treated all people equally. This rhetoric has been central in Liberation Theology, feminist critique, and queer advocacy, but it is highly problematic. As Judith Plaskow argued already in the 1970s, this interpretation relies on a selective reading not only of Jewish documents but also Christian sources in order to draw the most positive conclusions possible about Jesus (Plaskow 1978). Today, Amy-Jill Levine and other Jewish New Testament scholars are also underscoring the ways in which Jesus's highest values emerge from (rather than stand in contrast to) Jewish faith (Levine 2007).

COLONIZED PROPHETS

Without diminishing in any way the scale of and damage done by the anti-Judaism of nineteenth-century German historical biblical critics, I would suggest that their work has even wider ramifications. In making over the Bible to fit their preferred narrative, "scientific" biblical scholars colonized the Bible, co-opting it to serve their own interests through their characterizations not only of Jews but also of all others in the Bible and in their own world. For example, Paul Kurtz explores the way this theology shaped the field of archaeology in the early twentieth century, as German scholars flocked to the East *not* to learn about Israel's contemporary inhabitants but to retrieve evidence of the past—a past envisioned as their own. Having already written Jews out of this history of faith and already having cast the biblical past as an exotic "Orient," they romanticized Bedouins and Arabs as "primitives" whose customs (they claimed) had barely changed since the time of the Bible (Kurtz 2019, 71).

Orientalism, as Edward Said famously argued, is at its heart a view of Western superiority (Said 1979). While it appears to value the primitive as authentic and true, its core assumption is that the other is different and inferior. Such a view was already clear in the thought of Michaelis and Eichhorn at the source of the Göttingen pipeline, and eventually transparent in Eichhorn's hero Herder. Gunkel ostensibly praised the Orient, but he primarily employed it as a tool to affirm the truth of Christianity.

In the decades to follow, Jewishness would be drained not only from Jesus' religious teachings but also his racial *bloodline*. As Susanna Heschel explores in *The Aryan Jesus*, Paul Haupt, a student of Germany's leading Assyriologist, even tried to make Jesus racially Aryan by contending that he might have been descended from Assyrians sent to the Galilee (Heschel 2008, 57). "Rejecting Jesus' Jewishness and defining him as Aryan was about not only redefining Christianity, but racializing Europe: reassuring Europeans that they were white" (Heschel 2008, 28). This construction of whiteness would continue to have wide-ranging repercussions to newly imagined "people of color" facing European and English empires. "By converting to Christianity, blacks did not become white, any more than Jews became Aryans" (Heschel 2008, 28). Instead, they became exotic others whose beliefs, identities, and human worth would be constructed to fit and support a white Christian narrative. Modern man is a white man.

Paul Kurtz argues, convincingly I think, that the German scholars' preference for the earliest stages of Israel's history was not simply a philosophical matter but closely tied to German nationalism, which was itself closely interwoven with Germany's Lutheran soul (Kurtz 2021). He describes the ways in which prioritizing early sources and the Prophets over sources composed after Israel's loss of national sovereignty fit with the German equation of God, land, and nation. Late sources like P were not problematic simply because of their chronology but because they come from a period when the Jewish people (according to nineteenth-century German historians) were making concessions by accepting their lack of national independence. Kurtz also explains the ways in which the German scholars' fascination with Israel's history reflects their own sense of the role of Germany in God's purposes. "By studying the history of Israel, they hoped to learn the history of God" (Kurtz 2021). Israel's history, just like Germany's own history, revealed God at work through those whose faith was true.

Subsequent progressives have rightly critiqued the nationalism and racism of German scholars, and many of the most famous progressive voices deserve credit for their vocal challenge to dangerous ideologies. Fosdick asserted that "nationalism has been shown to be a Caesar, a false god which we have been worshiping and magnifying past all reason" (*Jewish Daily Bulletin* 1927, 3). For Rauschenbusch and Gutiérréz, the liberal characterization of prophecy fueled resistance to capitalism, and for Cone it provided grounds to challenge white supremacy. Yet progressive discourse about social activism continues to employ many of the racialized and Eurocentric tropes of the past. It privileges the rational, the universal, the intellectual, and those who see prophets as conforming to these values. It has reified a way of understanding prophecy that reflects Eurocentric values over other understandings.

Persistently, progressives describe alternative views of prophecy as not simply wrong but as naïve, uneducated, and superstitious—remnants of old, outmoded, traditional trends of thought. And yet in my experience, most progressive Christians hold only stereotypes of other views of prophecy, unaware of the nuanced ways in which the category of prophecy is utilized in other understandings of past and present phenomena. This is especially evident in the way that progressives often characterize the Pentecostal and Holiness belief in the ongoing gift of prophecy as the symptom of an uneducated gullibility that simply accepts what someone claims in the name of God. Yet while Pentecostalism does make the gifts of the Spirit central to the Christian life, supporting the possibility that contemporary people can receive divine messages, most Pentecostal traditions do not simply accept all claims made in the name of prophecy. For example, even in the early years after the Azuza Street Revival (widely recognized as the origins of the movement), criteria for prophecy were being articulated. Between 1922 and 1941, five prominent Pentecostal publishing houses distributed nine unique treatments on the discernment of spiritual gifts. These publications lay out criteria for true prophecy: the prophet must be meek, not accept money, edify the church, manifest a holy life, and—importantly—have received the baptism of the Holy Spirit, including the gift of tongues (Kay 2011, 127).

Although Pentecostalism has developed significantly since the early twentieth century, I heard many of these criteria repeated when I interviewed several pastors in my area. The pastor of a massive congregation that calls itself "continuationist" rather than charismatic celebrates prophecy and holds annual retreats in which individuals receive private prophecies, but the pastor insisted that a true prophecy must confirm what the Spirit has told others in the congregation and meet the scriptural standard of building up the body of Christ. "Prophecy has power, but we do not govern by prophetic utterance. We are committed to maintaining the tension between the objective word of God (Scripture) and subjective word of God (contemporary gifts of the spirit)" (private interview, 2017). A pastor of an African American Baptist church explained that while Baptists don't identify as Pentecostal, the discernment of claims to prophecy is a major issue in his congregation due to what he called the "bleeding" between denominations. His criteria for true prophecy were clear: a prediction must come true, the prophet must be a trustworthy person, and "if it's new, it's not true" (private interview, 2017). The Spirit will not give a word that goes against Scripture and has not been shared with others.

Both pastors also expressed great concern about modern charismatic movements such as the New Apostolic Reformation, which calls for reinstituting the offices of prophets and apostles and advances a clear conservative political agenda. The pastors did not accept the authority of these claims on the grounds that they operate outside of the church and are insufficiently scriptural. Along the same lines, in 2001 the General Presbytery of the Assemblies of God, a historic Pentecostal denomination, issued an official statement affirming that while the gift of prophecy may be widely shared among peoples of the Spirit, "The New Testament does not make provisions for establishing the prophet in a hierarchical governing structure of the church; in fact, the content of prophecy itself should always be tested by and responsible to the superior authority of Scripture" (Assemblies of God 2001).

These examples suggest that views of prophecy as privileged information, including about the future, are not always naively accepted as inherently true, yet progressives continue to describe any understanding of prophecy other than that of social justice advocacy as superstitious and "unscientific."

THE ORTHODOXY AS BOUNDARY WORK

Consistently, the progressive orthodoxy about the prophets has served the purposes of what sociologist Thomas Gieryn describes as "boundary work" (Gieryn 1983). In everyday settings as much as scientific research itself, the "scientific" is demarcated from the "unscientific" as a way of deeming the former of greater value and authority. When applied to the characterization of prophecy, Gieryn's framework reveals the ways in which progressive thinking has pitted "science," "scholarship," and "historical study" against "tradition," "faith," and "superstition": rationalist interpretations of the prophets are granted a seemingly objective validity while supernatural interpretations are uneducated and naïve.

The "boundary work" of biblical interpretation, of course, comes with high stakes. Privileging one interpretation of the Prophets over another is not simply an academic exercise, but a way of connecting the Prophets with one's own life. As Paul Kurtz expressed to me in an email, "This attempt to rationalize, to modernize the prophets is a conservative one: to keep them close, to preserve them—their relevance, and their teachings" (Kurtz 2022). Boundary work also explicitly or implicitly claims biblical authority for one's own values in opposition to competing values. After all, if the prophets and Jesus are social activists, then so too should be all Christians.

The dismissal of other understandings of prophecy runs rampant through the history of progressive thought. In his 1907 address to the National Council of Congregational Churches in which he extolled the prophets as social critics, Gladden mentioned the 1906 San Francisco earthquake but not the Azusa Street Revival, which newspapers around the country were covering. In 1914 Rauschenbusch asserted that spiritual gifts interest only

> the minds of the weak. . . . Religion for them begins beyond the boundary line of the normal and becomes the more divine the more abnormal it is. They take joy in yielding their emotions and their intellect to mysterious powers and abdicating the possession of their own personality in favor of uncontrollable psychic forces. . . . Paul did here (in 1 Corinthians 13–14) for religious emotionalism what Jesus did for the religious formalism of the Pharisees . . . Paul prefers religion plus reason to religion minus reason—a principle of immense practical importance. (Rauschenbusch 1914, 12–13, 16)

This same assumption of intellectual superiority runs through current academic and religious discourse, where those who might believe in prediction of the future—or at least that the Hebrew prophets once did so—are treated as "uneducated." Such is the approach of most Hebrew Bible textbooks that seek to explain that, contrary to popular wisdom, prophecy does not mean prediction. No discussion of alternative views, either of ancient Near Eastern prophecy or modern charismatics, is given credence.

As Gieryn points out, "The boundaries of science are ambiguous, flexible, historically changing, contextually variable, internally inconsistent, and sometimes disputed" (Gieryn 1983, 792). Applying the label to one's own position, in the case of prophecy and elsewhere, is not a simply factual label but serves an ideological and social function, while obscuring the dynamics of power. Far from a straightforward reading of the biblical texts, the view of prophets as "forthtellers not foretellers" is a traditioned way of reading the Prophets selectively.

Of course the "forthtellers not foretellers" orthodoxy doesn't do the work of marginalization alone. Rather, it is one of the dozens of boundaries created in education and popular thought that valorize some values and dismiss others. Even as trends in biblical scholarship increasingly critique the Enlightenment foundations of the discipline, orthodoxies such as this one continue to do their work of constraint.

ACADEMIC CONSTRAINTS

The imposition of the progressive paradigm of prophecy on the study of other historical movements likewise has flattened and overly simplified our understanding of their complexities. When all controversies are understood as the silencing of justice-oriented prophets by bureaucratic institutions, the details and dynamics of each are obscured.

In the study of the New Testament, the progressive orthodoxy has insisted that the historical Jesus was radically inclusive—championing the cause of sexual minorities, the poor, and women—but in the subsequent decades and centuries the emerging church blunted this message in favor of a bureaucratized religious system. For example, in her masterful 1983 work, *In Memory of Her*, Elisabeth Schüssler Fiorenza argued that Jesus treated women as fully equal partners in his ministry, intentionally seeking to overturn patriarchy. In the second century, however, the emerging church sought to control women, as typified in the teachings of 1 Timothy 2:11 for women to learn silently, in full submission.

Schüssler Fiorenza's volume, while still widely appreciated, has been challenged by its selectivity and its treatment of Judaism (Kraemer 1985); in fact, in later work Schüssler Fiorenza acknowledged the validity of many of these critiques. Today, it is striking that progressives continue to portray Jesus as a feminist, even as contrary voices point to the ways in which the Gospels fall short of a liberative attitude toward women (Levine 2019; Smith 2016) and call for a more nuanced understanding of second-century documents.

In chapter 2 I demonstrated that in Luke–Acts, Paul, and later movements such as Montanism, prophecy functioned in ways far different from social critique. Prophecy is important (and dangerous) for many other reasons than its critique of structures of oppression. And all definitions of prophecy, progressive as well as otherwise, serve particular interests.

UNDERSTANDING THE WORLD,
UNDERSTANDING OURSELVES

It would be easy to distance myself from the German, British, and U.S. male scholars whose work I have discussed in the last two chapters. I can point out the prejudices of Michaelis, Wellhausen, Duhm, Gladden, and Fosdick and credit myself with the conscious effort I have devoted to challenging their assumptions. Yet in studying these networks, I've also been able to see how this contact tracing reaches into my own life. The ideas of German scholars and the Social Gospel shaped not only the scholarship I had to master to obtain my degrees but also the teachers who sparked in me a fascination with the Hebrew Bible.

Closer to home, their assertions have wound through the only preaching that I heard for the first eighteen years of my life—from the pastor who was also my father, a 1947 graduate of Lancaster Theological Seminary, where I taught for twenty-seven years. Dad learned the Old Testament from Donald Englert, Professor of Hebrew and Old Testament Science (the same title received by Frederick Gast in 1904); Englert taught at Lancaster for thirty-seven years after completing postgraduate work in Germany and Switzerland. From my father's ministerial library, I inherited books by Fosdick and titles such as *The Modern Message of the Minor Prophets* (Calkins 1947). One volume—titled *Preaching from the Prophets*, in which Dad underlined more words than he didn't—lists the marks of the prophet as "an uncompromising individualist," "an outspoken critic of specific evils in the social order." The prophet is "an ethical teacher, a moral reformer, a dangerous disturber of men's minds," unlike the priest who is "apt to be a conservative who finds it difficult to worship God except by means of elaborate ceremonies and ritual observances" (Yates 1942, 3–4). I don't remember my father talking about the Prophets, but in retrospect I can see the powerful ways these images shaped me, alongside the progressive values I was learning in the United Church of Christ. In addition to a commitment to justice, I learned, as Willie Jennings describes it, to love the white self-sufficient man or at least the version of it that I could perform. I have spent a career increasingly resisting those impulses—and yet, and yet, they continue to frame my field and the collective psyche of Western education. The legacies of an academic orthodoxy crafted in the nineteenth century continue to influence me, as well as public political discourse and our ability to understand one another.

The use of the "prophets as activists" orthodoxy to promote social justice movements has done good. It has called attention to aspects of the prophetic books that tend to be overlooked by Christians when prophetic utterance is reduced to predictions of the Messiah. It has rightly resisted those who assert that God has given them power to tell others what to do. It has linked faith with justice in a way that inspires. Abraham Joshua Heschel was inspired to join the civil rights movement because of the prophets he had spent his lifetime studying. Martin Luther King Jr. was able to channel Amos's statements about "justice rolling down like waters" so effectively because, even though Amos is both more and less than about social justice, its poetry continues to resonate.

Yet this orthodoxy that only rational interpretations of reality are "educated" both restricts our understanding of the prophetic books but also limits possibilities of productive discourse in the present. Despite stereotypes, not all conservatives embrace the possibility of ongoing prophecy; particularly those with strong attachments to authoritative texts are skeptical that God can be known through one's own experience. Similarly, progressive Christians also vary widely in their claims about divine communication, with some seemingly open to all forms of individual experience but others approaching life and religious texts from a decidedly humanist and rational perspective.

My appeal is for us to get beyond the intellectual arrogance of slogans and simplistic binaries—about prophecy and about each other—to listen to the purposes for which various intellectual frameworks are being used and to ask about their intended and unintended consequences. It is also an appeal to take seriously that our own views are constructed, just as much as are the views of our opponents. Our views come from somewhere and aren't just "the way it is."

My ultimate goal in this work, however, is to open up space for other ways to interpret the Prophets. If we engage prophetic literature afresh, apart from foregone conclusions about what they did and said and why they matter, what can we find? How can the prophetic literature spark life-giving discussions about justice apart from the orthodoxy that they were the individual heroes of social justice? What new word can we hear when we listen to something other than our own voices?

In part 2 of this volume, I take up these questions in conversation with the details of the prophetic books and with their diverse interpreters. Each chapter focuses on an aspect of social justice and then explores in some detail the prophetic passages usually invoked as its champion. As I attempt to demonstrate, these texts do not have to be mirrors of our own views to enrich our justice engagements in the present. We can avoid biblical ventriloquism without abandoning our own commitments to justice.

PART TWO

New Approaches
to Justice and the Prophets

5

The Prophets and Economic Justice

Amos and Micah

If we listened only to social justice advocates, we would have little doubt about the message of the Hebrew prophets and the prophet Jesus. They preached justice. Social justice. And particularly economic social justice. In the early twentieth century, the Social Gospel proponent Walter Rauschenbusch stated it clearly: "The sympathy of the prophets, even of the most aristocratic among them, was entirely on the side of the poorer classes" (Rauschenbusch 1907, 11). For proof of his position, he cited the nineteenth-century German scholar Emil Friedrich Kautzsch, best known for editing the *Hebrew Grammar* of Wilhelm Gesenius (discussed in chapter 3). In the mid-twentieth century, the Latin American liberation theologian Gustavo Gutiérrez asserted, "The prophets condemn every kind of abuse, every form of keeping the poor in poverty or of creating new poor" (Gutiérrez 1988, 167).

It would be difficult to overstate just how pervasively the identification of the prophetic message with economic justice has run through Christian ethical discourse. It appears throughout popular statements and the official ethical statements of various Christian bodies. In the 1980s, progressive evangelicals such as Jim Wallis (founder of *Sojourners* magazine) and Ron Sider invoked Amos, Micah, and Isaiah against the economic policies of Ronald Reagan and George H. W. Bush: "Because the Hebrew prophets' condemnations of economic injustice shaped progressive evangelicals' theology of liberation, leaders invoked them as allies" (Brantley 2014). The 1986 pastoral letter by the United States Conference of Catholic Bishops titled "Economic Justice for All" repeatedly cited the prophets as grounds for modern economic parity and linked them solidly to the mission of Jesus, insisting that "Jesus, especially in Luke, lives as a poor man, like the prophet takes the side of the poor, and warns of the dangers of wealth" (National Conference of Catholic Bishops

1986, 13). In a 2009 resolution approved at the United Church of Christ General Synod, the denomination committed itself to reach out to those in a troubled economy based on the biblical foundations of Jesus' teachings and the prophets' words: "The prophets applied this covenant of care to all of Israel calling for distributive justice and demonstrated equity from the greatest to the least" (UCC 2009). Across denominational and seminary websites, discussions of economic justice and the Bible find precedent in Deuteronomy, Amos, Micah, and Jesus (Adams n.d.). In 2022 the World Council of Churches issued a statement entitled "Called to Transformation," which used the term "prophetic" over sixty times to depict social justice and refers to the "prophetic heritage of unmasking systemic injustice and defending the rights of the poor" (World Council of Churches 2022, 16).

Academic articulations of Christian ethics likewise regularly make these strong connections. For example, Daniel Finn's *Christian Economic Ethics* (a classic in the field) points to Isaiah, Amos, and Jeremiah not only as prophets but as "prophetic" voices "regularly recruited by the Lord to publicly criticize the people of Israel, and in particularly the wealthy. . . . [They] called the well-to-do of their day to break out of their own comfort and to respond to the grieving of the poor" (Finn 2013, 42).

Rousing statements in the prophetic books and in the Gospels do indeed address wealth, corruption, and poverty. Isaiah lambasts those who "join house to house, / who add field to field" (Isa. 5:8) and "ruin the poor with lying words" (Isa. 32:7). Ezekiel includes in its definition of a righteous person one who "does not oppress anyone but restores to the debtor his pledge, commits no robbery, gives his bread to the hungry and covers the naked with a garment" (Ezek. 18:7), and the book announces judgment on those who have "practiced extortion and committed robbery; they have oppressed the poor and needy and have extorted from the alien without justice" (Ezek. 22:29). According to the Gospel of Luke, when Jesus visited his home synagogue in Nazareth, he took upon himself the mission of the anonymous prophet who speaks near the end of the book of Isaiah: like the prophet, Jesus sought

> to bring good news to the oppressed,
>   to bind up the brokenhearted,
> to proclaim liberty to the captives,
>   and release to the prisoners.
>   Luke 4:17–18; Isa. 61:1

Yet as I seek to show, interpreting the words on the pages of the prophetic books is not as clear as social advocates may suggest. As I explained in chapter 2, the poetry of the Prophets tends to be evocative and associative, full of hyperbole and wordplay. Claims for what they are "about" not only differ but often go beyond the text itself. My claim in this chapter is that attending to the ambiguity of prophetic discourse calls us to get more honest about for *what* forms of economic justice we are advocating and *why*. If we are going to work toward a particular form of justice, we need to name and claim our position rather than assuming the Prophets say it all.

Because Amos and Micah are most frequently characterized as clearly demonstrating the prophetic concern for the poor, I devote two chapters to these key books. In this chapter I focus on the ambiguity of the material in these books. Through close readings of key passages and a look at how commentators have paraphrased them, I'll make the case that while the characterization of Amos and Micah as advocating for economic equity clearly has some biblical warrant, it is not the full story. We cannot simply quote these books as self-evident calls to social change, but we can consider how they serve as useful conversation partners in our own advocacy.

In addition to talking about the whole books of Amos and Micah, I also focus on two passages for my case studies:

> Amos 8:4–7   semicontinuous First Reading in the Season after Pentecost, year C
>
> Micah 2:1–5

AMBIGUITY IN AMOS

Amos's reputation as the premier prophet of social justice is widespread. Quite famously, Amos 5:24 was quoted by Martin Luther King Jr. in his culminating speech of the March on Washington for Jobs and Freedom in 1963. In addition, the title of an essay in *Huffington Post* is telling: "The Prophet Amos as a Model for Addressing Issues of Economic Justice" (Flippin 2012). Among biblical scholars, M. Daniel Carroll R. has written powerfully about the book's resonances within modern settings of injustice (Carroll R. 1992; 2020), and Blake Couey offers a listing of economic crimes that Amos outlined:

> Along with generalized denunciations of socio-economic injustice (e.g., 2:7; 5:7; 8:4), texts in Amos criticize specific exploitative practices with parallels in many historical periods: debt slavery (2:6; 8:6), possible sexual exploitation of workers (2:7), property confiscation (2:8), judicial corruption (5:10, 12), excessive agricultural levies (5:11), and economic fraud (8:5–6). (Couey 2021, 431)

The passage treated here, Amos 8:4–7, seems to be the most direct statement of the prophet's interest in economic justice. Some within the audience are accused of bringing harm to the poor and needy through their unjust business practices and coldhearted pursuit of financial gain. They are characterized as

> buying the poor for silver
>   and the needy for a pair of sandals,
>   and selling the sweepings of the wheat.
> Amos 8:6

This language is an extension of the imagery introduced earlier in the book, which describes Israel as facing punishment

> because they sell the righteous for silver,
>   and the needy for a pair of sandals—
> they who trample the head of the poor into the dust of the earth
>   and push the afflicted out of the way.
> Amos 2:6–8

Read as examples of negative behaviors, the passage seems to solidify Amos's commitment to justice for the poor and marginalized.

Many social justice advocates treat accusations in Amos as literal descriptions of what was happening in ancient Israel. In his volume on the eighth-century prophets, for example, D. N. Premnath finds evidence in Amos, Micah, and Isaiah for the economic realities of ancient Israel and Judah, tracing the "gradual deprivation of the peasantry" through the practice of latifundialization—the accumulation of land into the control of wealthy landowners (Premnath 2003, 43). He cites passages in Amos as indicators of the growth of urban centers (Amos 3:9–11; Premnath 2003, 109–11), taxation (Amos 5:11–12; Premnath 2003, 131–34), the luxuries of the elite (Amos 3:15; Premnath 2003, 136–42), corrupt market practices (Amos 8:4–6; Premnath 2003, 158–61), debt slavery (Amos 2:6–8; Premnath 2003, 162–66), and judicial rulings controlled by the elites (Amos 5:7, 10; Premnath 2003, 169–70).

Although these correlations between Amos's words and economic practices seem to be plain, commonsense readings, it is important to recognize the rhetorical dimensions of Amos's language. Indeed, Amos's literary style complicates determining exactly what behaviors are being critiqued. For example, while Premnath and others read the accusation that the oppressed are bought and sold for money and sandals (Amos 2:6; 8:6) as clear evidence of debt slavery, it is important to note that the wealthy do not themselves sell others into slavery. As described in Leviticus 25:39, Deuteronomy 15:12, 2 Kings 4:1, and perhaps Exodus 21:2–17, the mechanisms of debt slavery led desperate families to sell members to others in order to pay off creditors, such that the poor would have sold others into debt slavery because of their dire straits. By accusing the wealthy of selling people into debt slavery, Amos is making the case that their actions are *to blame* for the selling without explaining what prior actions of the wealthy led to their enslavement. Obviously, Amos is claiming that a group is harming the poor, but the particular details of their actions that led to debt slavery are not perfectly clear.

As I explained in more detail in chapter 2, throughout Amos (and the Bible), differing judgments about whether a particular passage is to be understood literally or metaphorically can change our understanding of what a passage actually "says." A prime example is Amos 5:21–24. Consistently, the nineteenth-century German scholars described in chapter 3 saw in Amos's claim that God hates religious festivals and sacrificial offerings clear confirmation of the inferiority of Judaism (which they defined as sectarian, ritualistic, and legalistic) to Christianity (which they defined as grounded in faith and ethics). For Wellhausen and many later Christians, Amos's rejection of sacrifices is a literal description of God's intentions. Other interpreters in the past and the present, quite to the contrary, have understood Amos 5 as claiming that God hates religious ritual *that is not accompanied by ethical practices*. Just as God *hates* the one who perverts justice in the public square (Amos 5:10), so too God *hates* hypocritical worship. What is literal for one interpreter is hyperbole for another, leading to very different outcomes. (A similar inconsistency between reading metaphorically or literally emerges when interpreters discuss Luke 14:26, in which Jesus insists that followers must "hate" family members and one's own life. Is this intended as an exaggeration about relative priorities or a direct challenge to patriarchal family norms?)

Claiming that Amos 8:4–7 is an obvious call for particular forms of economic justice also fails to acknowledge the hyperbolic nature of the "trampl[ing]" of the poor in 8:4 and its parallel passage in 2:7 (in the NRSV and NRSVue, "trample" also appears in 5:11, even though the Hebrew uses a different and unique verb). Few interpreters assume that the poor were literally being assaulted physically, recognizing that Amos is making a bold statement about the horrendous *effects* of the actions of their oppressors: the poor were subjected to "grinding" poverty, "buried" in debt. As in the case of "buying" the poor, the accusation that the wealthy "trample" the poor describes not their actual *actions* but the *results* of those actions, described in figurative terms. Moreover, the identities and specific economic status of those whom the book considers poor are not detailed, left faceless behind a generic label.

Another way of noticing the ambiguity of what Amos is *about* is to acknowledge that the book as a whole reflects a range of concerns. While references to the poor, the wealthy, and business practices are frequent, economics is not the book's only or even most central concern. Depending on how one interprets its poetry, the book may also critique forced deportations (Amos 1:9), war atrocities (Amos 1:13), mistreatments of a corpse (Amos 2:1), failure to observe traditional religious laws (Amos 2:4), prostitution or incest (Amos 2:7), worshiping outside Jerusalem (Amos 5:5), and the absence of the Davidic monarchy (Amos 9:11).

In pointing out these ambiguities, my intention is not to deny the power of Amos's rhetoric or to minimize the imperative of economic equity in the present. My goal instead is to underscore the role of the interpreter in prioritizing Amos's statements about the poor over other concerns of the book and in equating particular terms in the book to specific economic conditions in the past and present.

In chapter 6 I highlight other dimensions of the book of Amos as well— its failure to address structural change, the likely rhetorical intentions of its redactors, and the *injustice* that readers of various social locations have attributed to this apparent hero of ethics. Here I seek to underscore that the words of Amos themselves are less transparently clear than many progressive interpreters suggest. Progressives, as all interpreters, supplement (usually unwittingly) the words on the page.

AMBIGUITY IN MICAH

Almost as often as Amos, the prophet Micah is touted as advancing a message of economic justice. In the words of Rainer Kessler, "The main theme of the book of Micah is social critique" (Kessler 2021, 467). According to Delbert Hillers, "Micah speaks of the achieving of a social and religious ideal from which the covetous and their descendants will be excluded. The future 'assembly of Yahweh' will consist of the oppressed" (Hillers 1984, 33). In such circles, Micah's accusations against Judah are read as literal depictions of acts of economic injustice in ancient Israel: land and home seizure (Mic. 2:2), profit-seeking religious leadership (Mic. 3:5, 11), forced labor (Mic. 3:10), bribery (Mic. 3:11), and dishonest business practices (Mic. 6:11) (Kessler 2021, 467).

Yet even among those who read literally, disagreements arise about what actual crimes Micah claims are being committed and by whom. In his study of the prophets and economic justice, Matthew Coomber (Coomber 2010) describes some of the quite different economic situations that have been reconstructed from Micah's rhetoric.

1. The most common reconstruction simply pits "poor" against "rich" in ancient Israel. Coomber calls this the "ruthless businessman" motif, which

characterizes mistreatment of the poor by wealthy individuals as moti-
vated simply by greed. The haves are taking advantage of the have nots.

2. A variation of the first reconstruction draws close ties between the offend-
    ing wealthy individuals and the royal court. The former were able to ille-
    gally seize land because they were allied with corrupt judges. Accused
    people are not simply greedy individuals but also the structures of power
    that enable their predatory practices.

3. Other scholars have reconstructed the villains in Micah as members of a
    criminal cartel who were seizing the land of others. Rather than accusing
    the wealthy elite, Micah was accusing professional land-grabbers.

Coomber points out that none of these reconstructions finds solid grounding in Micah or in ancient history. The word "poor" (both the English word
and its Hebrew equivalents) doesn't appear in Micah, and the book offers no
reason to assume that the victims were in the class of "poor" before losing
their land (Coomber 2010, 12). In addition, the strength of the "state" at the
time of Micah (which Coomber sees as the eighth century) was minimal, and
there's no real basis for the reconstruction of a criminal network involved in
land seizure.

Coomber's own reconstruction, which has commonalities with the work
of Premnath mentioned earlier, instead situates Micah's rhetoric in a period
of profound structural change of the ancient Israelite economy from subsis-
tence farming to the development of large landholding estates. Rapid popu-
lation growth and the pressure posed by the taxation system of the Assyrian
Empire changed Israelite society as a whole, affecting not only the poor but
also all classes of society, including religious elites. Micah's complaints about
the loss of land and the collapse of traditional religious values would have
resonated not only with the poor (who are less likely to hold land, at any rate)
but with elites faced with changes in status: "members of various elite classes
can also suffer as the economic and social system upon which they depend for
status and revenue are overturned; as societies evolve, so do the institutions
upon which various groups depend" (Coomber 2010, 293). That is, Coomber
argues that those being championed in Micah were not the abject poor but
rather the average landholders whose livelihoods were being changed by a
new agricultural system. For this reason, he finds more ready comparisons
between Micah's audience and those today facing the realities of corporate
agribusiness than those who have lived a lifetime of poverty.

While Coomber's argument is more detailed and nuanced than I've described
it here, it is significant because it underscores the leaps that interpreters make
when they assume that the book of Micah advocates for the poor over against
the rich or lays out a program for distributive justice. When biblical commentaries provide concrete identification of victims and perpetrators, they "often

divulge more about the socio-economic world of the commentator than the period of the biblical text in question" (Coomber 2010, 8). Without denying the reality of poverty, it is also important to recognize that persons of various economic status can identify themselves as "poor" and rail against the "rich."

Such differences in defining what Micah 2:1–5 is "about" also are evident in the history of the interpretation of the passage. For example, in his eighteenth-century commentary, Matthew Henry stressed that the passage teaches the moral evils of covetousness (Henry n.d.). In a 2022 sermon, W. Pat Cunningham compared those who lost land in Micah to farmers who are today losing land due to "woke" environmental activism. Cunningham agreed that economic systems should be more just, but he defined justice as not imposing rules on farmers, since Jesus "came to change minds and hearts, not political systems" (Cunningham 2022). These readings clearly are quite different from those of the progressives and liberation theologians mentioned at the beginning of this chapter. Of course, interpreters in one theological camp quite easily dismiss the views of those of other theological persuasions, but a sampling of commentary on Micah underscores that what a book is *about* is rarely settled by simply citing verses from it.

TOWARD A MORE HUMBLE ACTIVISM

The very fact that Micah's and Amos's rhetoric regarding economic justice is open to multiple interpretations can be frustrating. These books do have powerful words against injustice, but they do not analyze the exact practices or spell out alternatives. Is it okay to have money as long as you don't trample the head of the poor into the dust of the earth but do give generously to the United Way? Is the solution to poverty charging fair prices for goods or distributing goods regardless of the ability to pay? Should initiatives to address economic disparity focus on crime, government corruption, or the morality of individuals?

Yet the ambiguity of these books is also a gift because it offers an invitation for more honest articulation of our own advocacy. As I've suggested throughout, one of the contributions of socially located, postmodern readings, such as those of feminists, womanists, and postcolonialist critics, is that they claim the agency of the reader. They call interpreters to step out from behind the cloak of presupposed neutrality and name the convictions, passions, and analysis that inform their interpretation. They insist that we must be clear about our questions, the context from which we work, and the convictions that animate our work.

In some ways, liberation theologians have undertaken this act of agency and transparency by naming their own preferential option for the poor and foregrounding their own social contexts as the vantage point from which they read. Yet in other ways, they, as most progressive interpreters, continue to claim the authority of the Bible for their perspectives: the prophets taught economic liberation, Jesus acted on behalf of economic liberation, and therefore economic liberation is mandated by Jesus himself. No less than conservatives, progressives have claimed that their own interpretations are the plain-text reading of the Bible, referring to "biblical ethics" or "biblical mandates" for social justice.

I am arguing that reading the Bible selectively and then claiming the authority of our reconstructions for our causes is not only dishonest but also unproductive to constructive activism. Until we acknowledge that biblical texts can be understood—and indeed have been understood—in different but equally legitimate ways, we will continue arguing about what texts say rather than about the assumptions and convictions that undergird these interpretations.

This is why I find advocacy, both from the pulpit and in the public square, most powerful when speakers begin with their analysis of the present. Given my own progressive acceptance of the validity of the sciences, even when their findings are debated, I want to hear social scientific analysis of the economic situation of my community and world and its causes. Then and only then am I open to hearing how the interpreter finds resonances with the biblical text.

An example of this kind of advocacy in my own context begins with the explanation of why in 2023 the Commonwealth Court of Pennsylvania ruled that the state's current school funding system is unjust. The state currently funds schools through the assessment of local property taxes, which means that schools in wealthy areas such as the suburbs receive far more funding than those in poorer areas. The result disproportionately affects Black and brown students: 20 percent of the poorest school districts educate 50 percent of the state's Black students and 40 percent of its Latinx students. The differential cannot be blamed on individual students or racial groups, since graduation rates for low-income students in wealthy schools are far higher than that of low-income students in poorer school districts (Fund Our Schools 2021).

When these forms of economic injustice are foregrounded, I find that Micah 2 resonates in complicated ways. I hear resonance with Micah's claim that those in power "oppress / people and their inheritance" (Mic. 2:2), but I also notice that Micah is almost exclusively focused on the rights of landowners, who in the modern context I've described find the most obvious parallel with those in wealthy districts protesting the "injustice" of having their taxes raised to educate other people's children. This recognition, in turn, allows me and those with me to move beyond statements about "justice" to ask important questions about the convictions we hold: How do our commitments to poor children of color and to wealthy homeowners compare?

Because Amos 8 focuses on business practices, I want progressive sermons and advocacy stands to start with analysis from outside of the religious community about, for example, the intersections between capitalism and the exploitation of workers in the fast fashion industry, in which 80 percent of contractors violated minimum wage standards in 2023 (Rosalez 2023). Consumer demand for inexpensive clothing is leading manufacturers to shortchange workers for the sake of profit. After this analysis, then and only then am I open to hearing how Amos's complaint that the needy are bought for a pair of sandals (Amos 8:6) echoes today—perhaps in an indictment of the abuse of child labor in the footwear industry and my own complicity in expecting shoes to be cheap.

That is, I don't need advocates for economic justice to use Amos or Micah to tell me what is wrong about my world or to provide biblical precedent for challenging those wrongs. I need them instead to find connections between the past and the present, and to explain how they are making those connections. I want them to do so passionately but also humbly, naming what matters to them and helping me see how their Christian faith shapes their convictions.

Such an approach, of course, will not change the mind of those who disagree. But then again, neither does arguing about what passages *really* mean. In my experience, honest and transparent engagements with the world and with biblical texts encourage communities to have hard but necessary conversations. I am convinced that we need fewer churches where everyone agrees with one another and more churches able to engage in dialogue across difference. Because each of us, including the most passionate advocate, has a limited view of justice, we need to talk to and rub up against each other in hopes of discovering both the values we share and also our own blind spots. In that way, Micah and Amos allow us to engage in greater justice, both for the world and for one another.

6

The Prophets and Structures of Oppression

Amos and Micah

One of the core convictions of contemporary social activism is that justice work must address *systems* of oppression. This is a theme, as we saw in chapter 3, that animated the work of the Social Gospel and early Liberation Theology. In the present, contemporary social activism involves not simply feeding the poor, but addressing the inequitable economic structures of poverty itself; not simply offering women or sexual minorities equal access to employment, but challenging the gender-based ideologies that constrain their success; not by simply feigning color-blindness, but unmasking the ideologies and public policies that create and sustain unequal treatment of persons based on particular constructions of "race."

In this chapter I focus on the challenges that prophetic books pose for those committed to the work of dismantling systems of oppression. While prophetic passages from Amos and Micah do inveigh against their societies, when these passages are read in the literary contexts of their books and the historical context of their redaction, their relevance to social change becomes less clear. Yet as I contend, they can continue to inspire readers to action. For my case studies I return to the books of Amos and Micah, given just how central these books are to the progressive discourse regarding the prophets.

I'll focus on two passages:

Amos 5:21–24   alternate First Reading in the Season after Pentecost, year A

Micah 6:1–8   Fourth Sunday after Epiphany, year A

There are perhaps no two more beloved and quoted passages from the Prophets than these. According to progressive discourse, these passages encapsulate the call for justice. They provide the remedy to the ills outlined in Amos 8 and Micah 2, discussed in the previous chapter. Rather than buy the poor for silver (Amos 8:6), people should "let justice roll down like water and righteousness like an ever-flowing stream" (Amos 5:24). Rather than seize the fields and houses of others (Mic. 2:1–2), they should instead seek "to do justice and to love kindness / and to walk humbly with your God" (Mic. 6:8).

Social activists frequently interpret these passages as calling for structural change. In the 1840s, various abolitionists invoked Micah 6:8's call to "do justice" (Gehr 2016), and in 1907 Rauschenbusch invoked Amos 5 as proof that the prophets were concerned with social ethics (Rauschenbusch 1907, 6). He deemed Amos "the first of the great social prophets" (Rauschenbusch 1907, 16). In the 1930s Fosdick invoked Micah 6:8 as a clear indication that the prophets were engaged in social, and not just individual, justice:

> The prophetic leaders of Israel were as much interested as any members of the nation in the success of the social group; the beginning and end of their thought was Israel redeemed, purified, and fulfilling her mission in the world. Their interpretation of what this involved, however, went far beyond meticulous legalism and ritualism into ethical insight and creative moral living, saying with Micah, "What doth Yahweh require of thee, but to do justly, and to love kindness, and to walk humbly with thy God?" The progress involved in this creative work of the Hebrew conscience was one of the supreme contributions to human life which the Old Testament records. (Fosdick 1938, 114)

More recently, the Economic Justice Covenant Program approved by the 2009 General Synod of the United Church of Christ appealed to both Micah 6:8 and Amos 8:4–6 as the basis for its engagement of systemic economic disparities:

> In the Hebrew Bible, Micah and all the prophets were clear: God wants society to be just, to be fair. According to Micah, God "requires" us to do justice. . . . Some of the inequities are the result of longstanding and systemic racism, sexism, and xenophobic fear of the stranger. Others are simply rapacious, not unlike Amos' searing prophesy [Amos 8:4-6]: unconscionably low wages, exploitation of workers with no recourse, unfair pricing of many necessities, the luring of the poor into unbearable debt, and the pillaging of the earth's resources. (UCC n.d. "Economic")

Various social agencies derive their name from these books, including the Micah Project, which supports impoverished children in Honduras (Micah Project n.d.). The Micah Movement, which addresses human trafficking, domestic violence, poverty, immigration, foster care, adoption, substance abuse, racial reconciliation, and suicide prevention, finds its inspiration in Micah 6:8:

"Over 2700 years ago, the prophet Micah gave voice to the downtrodden and exploited people of Judean society. His message is still pertinent today and directs our hearts and daily lives"(Micah Movement 2023).

WHAT DO MICAH AND AMOS SAY?

In the previous chapter I argued that in Amos 8 and Micah 2 the details are not clear about who was oppressing whom and how. I make a similar case here for the justice prescriptions of Amos 5 and Micah 6. Exactly what are the people supposed to do?

The first place to see this lack of clarity is by comparing English translations of these passages. The primary Hebrew term in question (*mishpat*) appears in Amos 5:24 and Micah 6:8. For the Amos passage, modern English translations are relatively consistent in offering "justice" as its equivalent (NRSVue, NRSV, CEV, ESV, NIV, NKJV, and JPS); a few outliers are KJV ("judgment"), NLV ("what is fair"), and NIRV ("treat others fairly). For Micah 6:8 the translation of *mishpat* varies more significantly:

> NRSV, NRSVue: do justice
> KJV: do justly
> NIV: act justly
> CEV: see that justice is done
> ERV (Easy to Read Version, Bible League International): be fair to other people
> NET and EHV (Evangelical Heritage Version): carry out justice
> GW (God's Word Translation, God's Word to the Nations Bible Society): do what is right

In both verses, *mishpat* is paired with another Hebrew noun. The second noun in Micah 6:8, *hesed*, is usually translated as "kindness" (NRSV, ESV, NLV, NRSVue) or "mercy" (NIV, KJV, NLT); other options include "goodness" (JPS) and "faithfulness" (NET). The Message offers a freer translation: "Do what is fair and just to your neighbor, / be compassionate and loyal in your love." Amos 5:24 pairs *mishpat* with *tzedekah*, which is regularly translated as "righteousness."

Throughout these translations of Amos 5:24 and Micah 6:8, accepted behavior is described through the use of abstract nouns with different English connotations. "Judgment" does not carry the same nuance as social justice, and "being fair" does not necessarily imply structural change. "Kindness" in modern parlance is often seen as gentle treatment, while "faithfulness" implies a constancy of allegiance. "Righteousness" can be viewed as individual piety as well as behavior deemed correct by particular definitions. "Carrying out justice" evokes scenes of judicial or extrajudicial punishment for crime. "Doing what is right," of course, is in the eye of the beholder.

The Hebrew terms themselves carry this range of meanings as well. *Mishpat* is used for legal rulings in Leviticus (e.g., 5:10; 9:16) and Deuteronomy (e.g., 7:12; 11:1), where it is often translated in English as "ordinances." It appears in the context of the divine warrior's judgment against enemies (Deut. 32:41) and the trial held for someone who has slain another (Josh. 20:6). Daniel Smith-Christopher contends that, in the Prophets, *mishpat* usually appears in the midst of withering social critique (Smith-Christopher 2021), yet the term rarely is accompanied by explanations of what justice entails. In Isaiah, for example, *mishphat* is a general value in 1:27 ("justice," NRSV, NRSVue) and also a ruling against the people in 3:14 ("judgment"). In Hosea, Ephraim's oppression is because he was "crushed in judgment" (*mishpat*, 5:11), though the people are called to hold fast to *mishpat* ("justice," 12:6). The word appears twice in Habakkuk 1:4, both for the complaint that "justice" never prevails and the "judgment" is perverted. In the larger context of the book of Micah, *mishpat* refers not only to "justice" that should be valued (Mic. 6:8) but also the act of God who "execut[es] judgment" for the sake of Israel (Mic. 7:9).

Running through all these nuances of *mishpat* is the sense of justice as a correct decision or course of action: a "right" action. While the act of ameliorating social ills such as poverty may indeed be understood as proper and valuable, attention to social *systems* such as economics, racism, or militarism are not built into the term itself. Even when Amos and Micah critique greed and land seizure, neither addresses the economic systems upon which they depend, including inheritance-based land ownership, patterns of commerce, or taxation by local or foreign powers (a possibility discussed in chapter 5).

WHAT ARE AMOS AND MICAH ABOUT?

As in the case of other chapters of these books, the diversity of modern interpretations highlights that not everyone agrees that Amos 5 and Micah 6 are about social justice. For example, one blog post on the Knowable Word website insists that, when read in the context of the book as a whole, Micah 6:8 points to the need for a messiah who would enact justice, mercy, and humility—predicting the precise type of Savior Jesus would be (Higginbottom 2020). A sermon help on Working Preacher, to the contrary, stresses that it teaches there is no difference between being spiritual and being religious (Oden 2011). As Couey explains, Obvious Vengeyi uses the book to challenge the "gospel of prosperity" in West Africa, a theology that blames Zimbabwe's extensive poverty on the sins of poor persons. Couey himself employs Amos in environmental ethics (Couey 2021).

Reading Amos 5 and Micah 6 within the literary context of their books and the historical context of their production likewise underscores that restructuring society was not the rhetorical aim of these books. Rather, both books seek to explain the reasons for Israel's destruction and to defend God's justification for doing so. Every criticism that Amos proffers is for the purpose of explaining the reasons for Israel's fall. Even when Amos does name economic abuses, it does so as preface to punishment. Amos 5 is in fact a lament over the imminent destruction of Israel; some scholars consider it a dirge. Israel's fall is so assured that it can already be lamented. God's call to "seek me and live" (Amos 5:4, 6), to "seek good and not evil" (Amos 5:14), and to "hate evil and love good, / and establish justice" (Amos 5:15) may seem to offer the possibility of repentance, but every imperative to change is followed by announcement of destruction. Amos 5:15–18 drips with the vocabulary of mourning, lamentation, and wailing, leading into the unit in which our passage is found; so do the sounds of wailing and mourning. Tellingly, the chapter ends with the declaration that the people will go into exile.

This pattern is also evident in Amos 8, treated in my discussion in the previous chapter. Amos does not call for change but for preparation for the destruction ahead: the announcement of Israel's end and ensuing death (Amos 8:2–3) precedes the accusations of the mistreatment of the poor (Amos 8:4–6), which in turn are immediately followed by the insistence that YHWH will not forget these sins (Amos 8:7). The book is consistent and insistent that the time for Israel's demise has come; its concluding expression of hope for a restored Davidic line and rebuilding of the ruins (Amos 9:11–15) looks toward a time beyond the present, after the inevitable destruction that God has decreed as punishment.

The significance of this explanation of Israel's exile becomes even clearer when we take seriously the historical context in which the book was put into its final form. In chapter 1 I discussed the likelihood that the prophetic books were edited or redacted in the fifth century or later to explain the destruction of Israel in the eighth century and the destruction of Judah in the sixth century. Finalized in retrospect, this literature insists that the destruction of both kingdoms was a righteous deity's justified punishment of those who failed to listen to the warnings of the prophets. The final form of Amos well serves this explanatory function. Its superscription would have explained to a postexilic audience that the eighth-century prophet Amos predicted the fall of the nation of Israel. The prophet foresaw that the women of Samaria would leave the city as exiles (Amos 4:1–4); that those in cities, farms, and vineyards would mourn (Amos 5:16–17); and that all would ultimately die even if taken into captivity (Amos 9:1–4)—predictions that, in retrospect, could be seen as confirmed. A postexilic audience would also have known about later events inferred in the final chapter of Amos: the fall of the Davidic monarchy (in the sixth century) and Edom's diminishment (likely in the sixth century, compare Mal. 1:2–5). The hope that the close of Amos offers, then, would apply to the "now" of the Persian period. Read in this context, Amos would have "taught" that Israel deserved its fate, just as the prophets of Jeremiah and Ezekiel claimed regarding Judah, a hope that would come after destruction.

Reading Micah in literary and historical context leads to similar conclusions. Although scholars disagree about how the book of Micah hangs together as a coherent whole, it can be read as following a trajectory. Micah 1 opens with a speech announcing that Israel and Judah face impending punishment: YHWH is coming to tread down the high places of the earth (Mic. 1:3), and Israel's capital, Samaria, will soon be made into a heap of stones (Mic. 1:6). The earth as a whole will suffer because of the guilt of Samaria and Jerusalem. Micah 2 recounts the offenses prompting this punishment: the wicked have seized land, oppressed homeowners, and driven women and children from their "pleasant houses" (Mic. 2:9). In Micah 3 the verdict is extended to Judah's capital: Jerusalem also will be made into a heap of ruins (Mic. 3:12). In Micah 6, YHWH takes Israel to court. Calling the mountains and hills as witnesses, YHWH recounts all the good things done for Israel, insisting that the deity has upheld the divine side of the covenant relationship. In Micah 6:6–8, YHWH mirrors back to the people what they regularly profess in a cultic form: they know that the deity calls not for child sacrifice and rivers of oil but for people to act justly. The people, however, failed to honor their prior commitment to do justice, to love kindness, and to walk humbly with their God. The ensuing punishment is named again: the city will be made into "a desolation" (Mic. 6:16). Micah 7 ends the book with lament and a plaintive appeal for YHWH to forgive.

Social activists tend to treat Micah 6:8 as an innovation of the prophet, but such values were regularly expressed in the ancient world. Calls to justice, righteousness, and faithfulness resonate throughout the Hebrew Bible, as does the priority given to proper treatment of other human beings over ritual requirements (Isa. 1; Amos 5; Pss. 40; 51; Prov. 15; 21; 27, etc.). Those who value the sacrificial system can also value righteousness and justice, as seen in Psalm 33, which convenes temple musicians to celebrate that YHWH "loves righteousness and justice" (Ps. 33:5). The covenantal requirements set forth in the Torah make no distinction between ethics and ritual, presenting all norms for Israel's behavior as commandments from YHWH.

When read in literary context, Micah 6:8 is not a radical new teaching of the prophet. These general values, as well as the insistence that proper treatment of others takes priority over ritual performance, were assumed to have been known by the ancestors and thus are the standard to which behaviors of the present generation are justifiably held. Their failures to observe these simple and self-evident norms leads to the punchline that concludes Micah 6: because you have not done justice (that you knew to do) "therefore I will make you a desolation" (Mic. 6:16).

Because Micah refers to the Babylonian exile (Mic. 4:10) and often alludes to biblical texts written long after the eighth century, many scholars argue that it was written or at least redacted in the Persian period (see my Micah commentary for a fuller discussion: O'Brien 2015). Not surprisingly, then, in its final form Micah functions rhetorically much like Amos. It explains why Judah was destroyed and it seeks hope for a time after that destruction. When read as a postexilic retrospective on the fate of Israel and Judah, Micah 6 becomes less of a program for economic equity than an explanation for why the nations fell. As I mentioned in chapter 1, Joseph Blenkinsopp has argued that the redactors' interest in theodicy was a later modification and perversion of the original social justice message of the prophets (Blenkinsopp 2006, xvii–xviii, 5), but other scholars have argued to the contrary that references to social justice in books such as Micah may have actually been the addition of redactors (Zapff 2017).

In Amos and Micah, economic injustice is explained as the cause of Israel's fall, but nowhere do the books offer a vision, much less a program, for alternative economic structures. Like other prophetic books, they do not propose ways of mitigating social ills but instead announce that nations would be punished for not honoring them (Zevit 2004, 192). Neither Amos nor Micah nor other prophets call for the restructuring of society in order to eradicate poverty. It is then ironic, as Walter Houston notes, that "Amos is remembered, not primarily as the prophet of the fall of Israel, but as the prophet of justice for the poor, even though the structure of his text serves the former end rather than the latter" (Houston 2008, 73). Readers, of course, can choose to prioritize the passages of Amos that are economically oriented, but granting them priority is a choice and not a matter of simply reading the text. It may be an ethical interpretive option but one that needs to be named and owned.

THE ROLE OF THE READER

Lifting up Amos and Micah as the paragons of inclusive justice also tends to gloss over the specific forms of injustice that diverse populations experience. One of the earliest critiques of Amos, as I noted in chapter 2, was that of the feminist writer Judith Sanderson. Sanderson pointed to the ways that Amos scapegoats women for the crimes of the nation even though it never attends to the gendered dimensions of poverty itself (Sanderson 1992). In the past as in the present, the poor are disproportionately female, and in the social structure of ancient Israel the widow was among the poorest of the poor. Rather than champion the cause of the most poor, "With the notable exceptions of 1:13 and 2:7, victims of injustice in Amos are overwhelmingly male" (Couey 2021, 432).

When read for race and ethnicity, Amos produces similarly mixed justice results. On the one hand, the book's opening chapters seem to hold other nations to ethical standards of warfare, suggesting an ethic of universal human rights. Yet on the other hand, Amos's true focus becomes clear by Amos 2:6, after which the rest of the book devotes almost all of its attention to Israel. Read sequentially, the oracles against other nations serve as the rhetorical buildup to the book's claim about Israel: if other nations face consequences, then clearly Israel deserves greater punishment due to its unique status. YHWH dispossessed and destroyed others on Israel's behalf (Amos 2:9–10) and has an exclusive relationship with Israel ("You only have I known / of all the families of the earth" [Amos 3:2]). In the context of the book of Amos, then, care for the poor is described not as a universal ethical value but the obligations of Israel's distinctive covenant with God.

A similar case could be made about the poor in Amos. The book certainly criticizes mistreatment of the poor, but does its critique actually benefit the poor? By insisting that all Israel will fall due to the sins of the wealthy, Amos does not offer hope to the economically disadvantaged. In the past as in the present, those with limited economic resources suffer most in times of national crisis. The poor will perish along with the wealthy. When read as an explanation of Israel's fall, Amos treats the poor as an object lesson rather than subjects to be empowered.

Social activists who cast Amos as the prophet of social justice often ignore that the book advances a theological worldview that many progressive Christians resist: a punishing God. Throughout Amos, YHWH is described as orchestrating drought, hunger, pestilence, death, and planetary devastation to punish people for wrongdoing. As seen in Amos 4:6–12, Israel's failure to recognize these natural events as divine warnings was a tragic failure, forcing YHWH to issue a final and irrevocable decree of captivity and death (Amos 9:1–9). I find it ironic that Christians who decry punitive religion and define religion as ethics continue to laud prophets whose primary message is that of justified punishment for sin. I also find it ironic that those who characterize Jesus as the loving alternative to an angry Old Testament God also characterize Jesus as heir of the prophets whose message is primarily punitive.

In the case of Micah, the situation is slightly different. In my commentary in the Wisdom Biblical Commentary Series (O'Brien 2015), I suggested that it is both refreshing and concerning that Micah mentions women less than do other prophetic books. Missing from the book are prolonged scenes of sexualized violence, such as those found in the books of Hosea, Ezekiel, Jeremiah, and Nahum, and accusations of women's blame for the nations' fate, such as found in Amos. Yet this imagery lurks beneath the surface, in metaphors and comparisons. In Micah 2 the weak are described with feminine forms (including the sheep in Mic. 2:12), and in Micah 4:6–7 the words for the lame, "those who have been driven away" and "those who were cast off," are all feminine participles. In Micah 4:8–13, feminized Zion faces public rape as the nations gaze upon her and threaten her with being "profaned" (Mic. 4:11). Her only hope lies with her redeemer YHWH and, based on my understanding of Micah 4:8, the deity's Davidic king. In Micah 4:13, the empowered Daughter Zion loses her feminine characterization and becomes instead a draft animal who treads the nations underfoot.

Also missing in Micah is attention to the gendered dimensions of the book's concern with the loss of land. Micah 2:9 does complain that women and children were cut off from their homes, but it complains in a way that uses their victimhood for rhetorical effect. The mistreatment of women and children, in the past and the present, is often evoked to generate sympathy even when the distinctive needs of women and children are not considered.

In the patriarchal system of ancient Israel, women would have been dependent on male property owners for their survival, so the loss of land would have concerned them as well. Crosscultural comparisons indicate that in patriarchal societies where wealth is tied to land holding, land-poor families often struggle to provide adequate dowries for daughters to enter a "good marriage." In West Bengal, for example, these girls are "subject to neglect, gender-based violence, malnutrition and human trafficking, primarily due to poverty caused by landlessness. . . . Poor families often have a financial incentive to wed their daughters early to avoid dowry or offer them as maids so the girls can earn their dowry" (Schultz 2013). In the hopeful vision of Micah 4:4–5, men flourish: "they will sit, a man under this vine and under his fig tree" (a.t.), and "all the peoples walk, a man in the name of his god" (a.t.), but what the future holds for women is not named. By focusing on land rights, Micah leaves in the shadows those not privileged enough to own land—the abject poor, orphans, and women.

USING THESE BOOKS TODAY

These books are immensely inspiring. Through the power of their rhetoric, they not only express but provoke emotion. Even David Clines, who is quite skeptical about Amos's value in the present, acknowledges that the language of Amos expresses deep emotion: "There is undoubtedly a great deal of anger in [Amos 6:4–7] against the rich in Samaria, and its spirit of denunciation against idleness and luxury strikes a chord with democratically minded and hard-working readers" (Clines 1995, 78). In my estimation, that is actually the point of Micah and Amos: to generate anger at wrongdoing.

As this chapter and the previous one have underscored, the poetry of Amos and Micah does not provide a transparent window into ancient Israel's sins and its remedy. What they *do instead* is move the reader's emotions, provoking outrage and consent. The question posed in Micah 6:7 "Will the LORD be pleased with thousands of rams, / with ten thousands of rivers of oil?" is not one for which an answer is expected and certainly not an accurate description of Israel's sacrificial system. Rather, as a rhetorical question it sets the reader up to accept Micah's ethical statement, which is stated in simple syntax and thus seems self-evident common sense. The same may be said of Micah 2, discussed in the previous chapter. In Micah 2 the poetry paints a picture of coldhearted luxury and deserved punishment. The wealthy lie awake in bed, hatching plans that they execute as soon as the sun comes up. They strip off the clothes of the poor and leave women and children homeless. As punishment, evil will be placed on their necks like a yoke, and they will be penned in by YHWH like sheep in a fold. Throughout Micah 2:1–5, wordplay draws direct connections between action and consequence: because they devise wickedness and evil (Mic. 2:1), YHWH will devise evil against them (Mic. 2:3); because they seize fields (Mic. 2:1), they will lose fields (Mic. 2:4); because they rob a man's inheritance (Mic. 2:1), they will lose their right to allocations of ancestral inheritance (Mic. 2:5).

In considering again the way that modern activists employ Amos and Micah, we can recognize many of the same dynamics at work. Like the books themselves, speakers invoke these powerful words *in the context* of a larger speech or movement that makes their application to matters of justice clear. The biblical passages add passion and resonance to a call to action rather than define the action itself. The application of their rhetoric to the speaker's own values gives the books their "meaning."

This is why, I believe, invoking Micah 6:8 and Amos 5:24 is so common and so effective. These are moving passages. They inspire us. In Martin Luther King Jr.'s famous speech during the March on Washington, for example, the resonance of Amos's call to "let justice roll down like waters" helped stir King's audience. David True provides other examples of speakers invoking the persuasive power of prophecy for the sake of causes of justice, such as Frederick Douglass, who appealed to Isaiah and Jeremiah to condemn slavery (True 2021, xiv).

Walter Houston, a biblical scholar committed to justice, claims that the most enduring legacy of the Bible as a whole is exactly this function: not its laws but its vision and ability to shape and reshape our moral imagination (Houston 2008). He agrees that Micah isn't a social justice advocate according to modern definitions, but these prophetic speeches can invigorate our work.

The danger of inspiring rhetoric, of course, is that it can be used for any cause. Indeed, the more general the language (about justice, about righteousness), the more widely it can be co-opted. In the decades since his death, for example, King's soaring refrain of "I Have a Dream" has been invoked to tame his message and erase the political and economic import of his larger speech. This is true, too, for these beloved passages from Amos 5 and Micah 6: they can be used to inspire all kinds of things.

As such, I link my conclusions in this chapter with those from chapter 5 to ask a key question: How can modern social justice advocates draw from the inspirational power of the Prophets without explicitly or implicitly claiming biblical authority for our specific vision of justice? How can we inspire but remain humble about the limits of our own vision?

One fruitful way of maintaining the creative tension between these poles is to continue to listen to the voices of diverse interpreters, particularly those from diverse social locations. They not only help us recognize that these books do not provide the details of justice or an all-inclusive justice but also challenge us to consider whose justice our own advocacy denies in the present. Where do racism and gender bias cloud not only Amos's and Micah's visions of justice but also our own? How do we, like the prophetic authors, fall short of living up to our most lofty professions of faith? And how can we continue to be inspired by our vision of what we believe God has called us to be and do?

Like the audience of these authors and perhaps the authors themselves, we might be both chastised by our failure and inspired by what God has called us to be and do. Just and humble.

7

The Prophets and Inclusive Justice

Isaiah (and Luke)

As I explored in chapters 2 and 5, interpreters from various social locations have transformed biblical studies by pointing out the unspoken assumptions of power that animate texts and their readers. Those paying attention to gender, sexuality, class, race, and other socially constructed ideologies ask pointed questions about who benefits from particular ways of perceiving reality. As ethicists insist, justice is not a self-evident category. Few people would argue *against* justice, but they do disagree about whether a given policy or vision *constitutes* justice. I have learned this myself not only by engaging feminist scholars but also womanist and queer ones who point out the injustice in my own visions of justice, and from Indigenous and other minoritized readers who can see what my white privilege does not. Claims to the universal too often mask the particularities of inequity—how what is posed as good *for all* benefits *some more than others*. Whose justice does prophetic rhetoric actually promote? Attending to this question helps social activists avoid the myopia of defining justice on their own terms.

In this chapter I focus on the grand visions of the future offered in beloved passages of the book of Isaiah. While often extoled by activists as the ideal future, I suggest that careful reading of these passages calls for more careful attention to our hopes and dreams. For my case studies, I focus on two passages from Isaiah and offer brief consideration of a third:

Isaiah 2:1–5	First Advent, year A // Micah 4:1–5
Isaiah 61:1–4, 11	Third Advent, year B
Isaiah 58:1–12	Ash Wednesday, years A, B, and C;
	Fifth Sunday after Pentecost, year A
(Isa. 58:9b–14)	(Proper 16, year C)

Since the 1800s, it has been common to assign these chapters from the book of Isaiah to different authors and time periods. Isaiah 1–39 is typically designated as First Isaiah and understood to reflect the work of the historical prophet Isaiah in the eighth century BCE. Chapters 40–55 are considered Second Isaiah or Deutero-Isaiah, seen to reflect the hopes of the Judean community exiled in Babylonia in the sixth century. Chapters 55–66 are understood as Third Isaiah, the work of anonymous author(s) working in the fifth century, after descendants of those exiled from Jerusalem to Babylon repatriated to their ancestral homeland. Such delineations are still generally helpful, since these sections of the book do reflect different concerns. Most scholars today, however, recognize that the entire book of Isaiah underwent extensive redaction over time: the current shape of First Isaiah is as much a reflection of later periods as is Third Isaiah. Isaiah 2, 58, and 61 in particular are usually assigned to the final stages of the book's production, likely in the Persian period. As I explore, all three chapters presume Jerusalem's current devastation and express hope for Jerusalem's (re)turn to world prominence.

Social activists have variously appropriated these passages. All three offer both more and less than a call for social change.

ISAIAH 2:1–5

Antiwar activists have widely characterized Isaiah 2:1–5 as a vision of world peace, in which conflict between nations ceases and all join in mutuality. Christian pacifists commonly cite Isaiah 2 as key evidence that nonviolence is God's intention for humanity, as seen in its frequent occurrence in the work of the Mennonite pacificist John Howard Yoder (Yoder 2020). The image in Isaiah 2:4 (paralleled in Mic. 4:1–7) of swords being beaten into plowshares and spears into pruning hooks has been invoked for various attempts to mitigate violence. The image has inspired powerful works of art, not only the well-known sculpture that stands in front of the UN headquarters but also the massive plow fashioned from three thousand disabled handguns created by Esther and Michael Augsburger, now located on the campus of Eastern Mennonite University (Jefferson 2017). U.S. presidents including Richard Nixon, Jimmy Carter, and Ronald Reagan have appealed to its aspirations, and the Plowshares Movement, founded by eight pacifists including Daniel and Philip Berrigan, promoted resistance against nuclear war in the 1980s (Wikipedia n.d.). A San Francisco Bay area program to support veterans' transition from combat to civilian life has the name Swords to Ploughshares, and an organization in the northeastern United States devoted to mitigating gun violence paraphrases Micah in its goal of "transforming guns into garden tools" (Swords to Ploughshares Northeast n.d.).

Despite these assertions that Isaiah 2:1–5 expresses a vision of universal and inclusive nonviolence, however, the literary context of the passage makes clear that its focus is on the fate of Jerusalem. Immediately preceding these promises is an extended and scathing judgment on Judah: the people are compared to sons who continue to rebel despite parental beatings (Isa. 1:2–6), and the land is described as desolate. Jerusalem is called daughter Zion (Isa. 1:4, an image of abjection) and then a prostitute (Isa. 1:21; more scandalously accurate for the Hebrew term is the NRSV translation "whore"), and Judah is compared to Sodom and Gomorrah (Isa. 1:10). Because of their sin, YHWH will refuse to hear the people's supplications and will turn against them (Isa. 1:25).

Isaiah 2:1–5 offers the hope for a time *after* this stark, metaphor-filled litany of judgment. While Judah now faces judgment, "in the days to come" (Isa. 2:2), things will be different, almost utopian. The nations are envisioned as streaming to Jerusalem; those that do not currently acknowledge YHWH's sovereignty soon will accept the universal rule of Judah's deity. In this vision of world dominance, all bow to YHWH and accept Jerusalem and its Temple as authoritative. As Burkhard Zapff describes the parallel image in Micah, "Zion assumes the former role of the world capital Babylon as religious center" (Zapff 2022, 129). The cessation of conflict between nations is for the benefit of Judah, as Zion becomes the center of the world. Description of the painful realities of the current punishment, however, resumes immediately in Isaiah 2:6. Because of their idolatry and pride, the people will experience a devastating day of the LORD, in which YHWH will remove food, water, religious and political leaders; women (and Jerusalem as a metaphorical woman) will be debased; and men will fall in battle.

Indeed, the insistence on Judah's punishment dominates Isaiah 1–39. While Christian interpretation of First Isaiah tends to focus on the hopeful promises of Immanuel in Isaiah 7, a "Wonderful Counselor" in Isaiah 9, and a shoot from the stump of Jesse in Isaiah 11, the majority of the collection is devoted to scathing critique. Most pointedly, Isaiah 8:6 claims that YHWH will use the Assyrian Empire, the major Near Eastern superpower of the eighth century BCE, to punish Judah for not trusting in divine protection. Isaiah 10:5 uses a metaphor in explanation: Assyria is YHWH's club for destroying Judah. Ultimately, YHWH will punish the Assyrian king himself (Isa. 10:12), but not until all divine punishment of Jerusalem is completed. While beautiful words in Isaiah do offer words of hope, hope is envisioned as coming after destruction. Isaiah 2:1–5, then, is an oasis in a sea of judgment, a hope for an alternative future in contrast to the current reality.

The case is similar for the parallel passage in Micah 4:1–7. In Micah's version of the vision, Micah 4 resolves the judgments of Micah 1–3: Jerusalem, brought to trial in Micah 1 and sentenced with destruction in Micah 3, now is promised exaltation. The Micah passage differs somewhat from Isaiah, adding that in the future "they shall all sit under their own vines and under their own fig trees " (Mic. 4:4) and, following the image of nations streaming to Jerusalem, a depiction of the other nations' defeat. As I explained in chapter 7, in Micah 4:13 the newly empowered Daughter Zion is pictured with horns of iron and hooves of bronze, treading the nations underfoot as if they were grain on a threshing floor.

In Isaiah as well as in Micah, the submission of nations to Zion can go hand in hand with YHWH's punishment of them. While Isaiah 2 might be read as welcoming the nations, its parallel in Isaiah 66:1–13 makes clear that the submission of the nations serves to enrich Jerusalem. When Zion is vindicated, YHWH will give her "the wealth of the nations like an overflowing stream" (Isa. 66:12); those who return to Jerusalem will be comforted (Isa. 66:13) at the expense of others. A similar vision appears in Isaiah 45:14, where the wealth of Egypt, the merchandise of Cush, and the Sabeans (strikingly, *they* are mentioned rather than their possessions) come to Jerusalem in chains and bow down to its inhabitants, confessing the truth of Israel's god.

This vision of the exaltation of Jerusalem and others' recognition of its status is most helpfully understood within the historical context of the early Persian period, during which this passage was likely added to the book. In the sixth through fourth centuries BCE, the Persian province of Yehud was neither politically nor economically independent. Persians appointed its governors and demanded the paying of tribute to the imperial treasury. Even when the Temple was reestablished in Jerusalem in the sixth century, it operated under Persian control. "The [local] temples were important to the Persian imperial government for their use as mechanisms of social control and possibly as custodians of imperial financial interests in their local areas (district or provincial)" (Cataldo 2009, 184). The so-called Second Temple was not the independent, glorious shrine of Israel's past, as the account in Ezra 3:7–13 indicates. The difficulties of this era are reflected in Nehemiah 5, which names the dual pressure of Persian demands and crop failures, and in Joel 1:17–20 and Haggai 1:6–11, which describe food insecurity due to famine, drought, and pests.

Along with other passages in Isaiah as well as Zechariah 1–8 and Haggai 2:20–23, Isaiah 2 envisions the exaltation of Jerusalem as a time of restored pride and glory; those of many nations will recognize the sovereignty of Israel's god, and Judah will never again experience the ravages of war; in the hopes of Zechariah, "Many peoples and strong nations shall come to seek the LORD of hosts in Jerusalem and to entreat the favor of the LORD. Thus says the LORD of hosts: In those days ten men from nations of every language shall take hold of a Jew, grasping his garment and saying, 'Let us go with you, for we have heard that God is with you'" (Zech. 8:22–23). To its Persian-period audience, the book of Isaiah explained that while YHWH had orchestrated the past Assyrian oppression of Judah, YHWH also had promised the restoration of Jerusalem—a restoration that might yet materialize in their own time. Just as some modern millennialists read the predictions of the Bible as soon to be realized in their own lifetimes, so too this passage may have been heard in the Persian period as indication that the chasm between Jerusalem's current reality and its true destiny would soon be closed. Hold on; victory will soon be ours.

Read in a literary and historical context, then, Isaiah 2 is clearly far less universal than activists claim. Its goal is not universal equality or the "brotherhood of man" as early progressives touted but instead a peace that comes on Judah's terms. Conflict will cease when everyone accepts the truth of the author's religious convictions.

ISAIAH 61:1–4, 11 AND ISAIAH 58:1–12

These two passages from Third Isaiah seemingly encapsulate the causes of progressive activism. In Isaiah 61, an individual anointed by YHWH announces good news to the oppressed, the release of prisoners, comfort to mourners, and the repair of ruined cities. The proclamation of "the year of the LORD's favor" (Isa. 61:2) alludes to the year of Jubilee (Lev. 25:8–17), during which debts are canceled and land is returned to its ancestral holders. Similarly, in Isaiah 58, YHWH's intentions are outlined as freeing the oppressed, feeding the hungry, housing the homeless, and clothing the naked. In these two passages, economic justice, criminal justice, housing justice, and care for the human spirit are joined together in the work of the faithful.

These passages are perhaps most well known because, in addition to their regular appearance in the Revised Common Lectionary, they also are echoed in another passage that social activists embrace: Jesus' sermon in his hometown synagogue. In Luke 4:14–21, the words that Jesus reads from the scroll of Isaiah are a combination of Isaiah 61:1–2 and Isaiah 58:6 as found in the Septuagint translation (which adds "recovery of sight to the blind"). Jesus not only affirms the values expressed in Isaiah 61 and Isaiah 58 but also declares, "Today this scripture has been fulfilled in your hearing" (Luke 4:21). The priorities set forth in these passages define Jesus' mission in Luke.

Within progressive Christianity, that mission is defined as one of social action. According to progressives, Jesus did not address matters of individual piety but rather the societal inequities under which people live. As I explained in the introduction and chapter 4, progressives consistently describe Jesus as following in the footsteps of the prophets but outpacing them in challenging sexism, racism, poverty, and ableism: explicitly affirming women, foreigners, the poor, the blind, and the lame. For Christian activists, then, much is at stake in reading Isaiah 61 and Isaiah 58 as proof that action on behalf of social justice is (and always has been) the call of God: if social action is what Jesus taught, then surely his choice of text for his first sermon must affirm the same progressive values.

Indeed, progressive voices frequently cite Isaiah 58, Isaiah 61, and Luke 4, singly and in combination. All three passages appear in the entry on "Roots of Catholic Social Teaching" in the *New American Bible*, linking Jesus's message with the prophets and explaining that "through their powerful witness the prophets nourish and inspire Catholic Social Teaching on the preferential option for the poor, workers' rights, and justice and peace" (Colecchi n.d.). A listing of ninety-five passages indicating God's preferential option for the poor includes Luke 4, Isaiah 58, and Isaiah 61 (Smith 2023). Luke 4 is invoked as a call for the liberation of the marginalized in Nigeria (Uwaegbute 2019), and Isaiah 61 is touted as a motivation for Africans to combat human trafficking, violence, and government corruption: "a greater realization of Isaiah 61 in Africa hinges on Africans fighting injustice" (Cox 2019, 133).

Such interpretations mark the continuation of a long trend in progressive thinking characterizing Jesus as the heir of the prophets' emphasis on morality and social justice. In these modern voices can be heard echoes of Fosdick and Rauschenbusch, the latter who affirmed, "A comprehension of the essential purpose and spirit of the Prophets is necessary for a comprehension of the purpose and spirit of Jesus and of genuine Christianity," which he defined as "the righting of social wrongs" (Rauschenbusch 1907, 3, 5). Echoes also resonate of Cone, who claimed that "the prophetic tradition in which Jesus stood unambiguously is upon God's unqualified identification with the poor precisely because they are poor" (Cone [1970] 2010, 110), and Gutiérrez, who insisted that "the Kingdom and social injustice are incompatible" (Gutiérrez 1988, 97). According to the religious educational curriculum *Living the Questions*, "Jesus was a troublemaker. He said and did things that were upsetting to agents of the political and religious domination systems that oppressed the weak and downtrodden. In this way, Jesus stood firmly in the tradition of the prophets of Hebrew Scripture—those who offered a clear and challenging 'alternative script' to the status quo" (Kung 2007). Jesus, like the prophets, stood in opposition to his culture.

A concern with the injustice of social ills does indeed animate Third Isaiah. In the larger chapters from which the lectionary selections are taken,

YHWH's love of justice is negatively contrasted with YHWH's hatred of robbery and wrongdoing (Isa. 61:8), and added to the concern for the poor, hungry, unhoused, and naked are the rights of workers (Isa. 58:3). In Isaiah 56:1,
YHWH insists that people must do justice (paralleled with "what is right"),
but Isaiah 59 presents an extended complaint that justice is lacking (Isa. 59:8,
9, 11, 14, 15).

While concern with justice runs throughout all of Isaiah, Third Isaiah's justice rhetoric is distinctive from the rest of the book. Unlike Second Isaiah,
which announces YHWH's intention to comfort and restore Jerusalem, Third
Isaiah makes national well-being conditional on practicing justice. Such condi-
tionality is evident in Isaiah 58:6–14: *if* (and only if) the hearers engage in acts
of justice, *then* (Isa. 58:10) YHWH will grant them heritage of the ancestors.
While in Isaiah 9:2 all of the people who walked in darkness are granted light,
in Isaiah 58 only those who feed the hungry will see light. The current failure
of YHWH to act on their behalf is not due to YHWH's weakness but "Rather,
your iniquities have been barriers / between you and your God" (Isa. 59:2).

This prioritization of justice may cheer modern social activists, but when
Third Isaiah is read in literary context, the justice for which the author(s) advocate does not include everyone. Increasingly as the collection develops, salvation is limited to a subgroup within the community. The "servants" of YHWH
receive good things, while those called the "wicked" or sometimes simply "you"
are destined for punishment. Isaiah 65 well encapsulates this dichotomy. Only
"my servants" will inherit the divine promise (Isa. 65:9), unlike the "you" who
forsakes YHWH (Isa. 65:11ff.). In a litany of contrast in Isaiah 65:13–15, the
servants will eat, drink, rejoice, sing, and be given a new name, while "you" will
suffer the opposite. The book of Isaiah ends by promising differing futures for
YHWH's servants and YHWH's enemies, accusing the latter of idolatry and
envisioning them suffering in eternal fire (Isa. 66:14–24). On a less dramatic
note, Isaiah 57 promises that those who take refuge in YHWH will possess the
land (Isa. 57:13), but "There is no peace . . . for the wicked" (Isa. 57:21). When
justice is done, one group and not the other will benefit.

Identifying these groups has generated great debate. Some argue that the
acrimony is between those who remained in Jerusalem during the Babylonian
period and those who returned from forced deportation (Brett 2020), while
others understand them as distinct priestly groups with differing understandings of the proper workings of the Jerusalem religious cult (Hanson 1995;
Berges 2017). One proposal suggests instead that these were not preexisting
groups but categories intentionally created by Third Isaiah to denigrate those
with whom the author disagreed (Middlemas 2011). In all of these scenarios,
Third Isaiah drips with the pain of a fractured community, one that has abandoned the hope of national solidarity in favor of the hope for vindication. Of

course, in this description of the polarized community, Third Isaiah's author(s) identify with the oppressed servants and deem others as the wicked (Isa. 65:23).

In the servants' vision of justice, however, it is not only the out-group within their community who is excluded; so are those outside of the community. In Isaiah 61:5, strangers and foreigners become laborers who serve, and the wealth of the nations comes to those who receive good news and comfort (61:6). As in Isaiah 2, the focus throughout Third Isaiah remains on the vindication and exaltation of Jerusalem. It is Jerusalem whose light shines and who receives the nations' wealth in Isaiah 60:1–7, along with the return of her inhabitants. In Isaiah 62, Jerusalem's vindication is YHWH's sole focus; characterized as a woman, Zion alone is restored and vindicated.

When progressives universalize the message of Isaiah 58 and Isaiah 61, they necessarily downplay the specificity of these passages. The texts' calls for justice and care of the oppressed take precedence over their interest in the political exaltation of a particular place, the acrimony not only encouraged but perhaps also created between groups within the community, and the vindication demanded against those who disagree. These passages do call for justice, but at a cost.

While a full study of Luke is beyond the scope of this volume, it is helpful to recognize that the invocation of Isaiah 61 and Isaiah 58 in Luke 4 likewise is less of a model for universal social justice than progressives suggest. Most scholars recognize that the author of Luke has moved this episode to early in the Gospel (compared to Mark 6:1–6 and Matt. 13:53–58) and added unique material in part to amplify the tension between him and the Jewish community: only in Luke does Jesus' message of inclusion of the Gentiles provoke the people's rage and attempts at violence (Luke 4:28–30). As my New Testament colleague Greg Carey explains, Luke as a whole can be understood to include anti-Jewish sentiments, and the author's advocacy for the poor is often overstated: the audience of Luke seems to be the wealthy, for whom discourse about the poor serves as a warning (Carey 2017, 12–14). In addition, not all feminists find the teachings of Jesus in Luke (or the other Gospels) liberative (Corley 2014). Clearly, all biblical passages (including those describing Jesus' mission) require careful and honest interpretation.

WHOSE JUSTICE TODAY?

This same type of "peace and justice on my terms" thinking that runs throughout Isaiah has marred progressive movements for centuries. While progressives have been vocal critics of missionaries who seek to convert others to the Christian faith, they nonetheless have worked for a future of their own envisioning. In retrospect, it is easy to identify the imposition of "democratic" values on other countries; the silencing of female and LGBTQIA voices in the movement for civil rights; the inordinate privilege given to individualism and independent thought in Western education; the denigration of charismatic Christianity as superstitious rather than rational; the insistence that the Bible should only be read through rational, historical lenses; and so on. One of the charges brought against modern progressives, including by those within our ranks, is that policies often proposed as beneficial for all instead reflect the interests and biases of those in charge. In a 2023 *New York Times* interview, for example, multiple journalists discussed the ways in which policies designed by progressives to support the U.S. working class often come with restrictions out of touch with most people's lives, such as the restrictions on student loan forgiveness that require small business ownership in a disadvantaged community for three years (Leonhardt 2023).

In his study of the Minor Prophets, Jeremiah Cataldo offers a pointed postcolonial critique of common readings of passages that envision the restoration of Jerusalem. He argues that interpreting these texts as a timeless theological vision is an act of imperial appropriation. In the ancient world, this promise was political, "the reestablishment of sociopolitical institutions within the community . . . a renewed, or restored, independent kingdom of Israel/Judah" (Cataldo 2021, 344). Making the passage into a vision *for us*, he argues, replaces ourselves as heirs of the promise:

> The inherent risk—and common tendency—is that modern theological interpretations . . . tend to transform those communities into reflections of an idealized community consistent with theological interpretations of a restored "Body of Christ" or "Israel." Put differently, we tend to read in the "community" of Israel the theological ancestor of our own theologically defined communities. (Cataldo 2021, 343)

The concrete realities of other people are replaced as we become God's people, and our own aspirations about war overwrite ancient hopes for political autonomy.

Such appropriation of these passages for the present also feeds into Christian tendencies to de-Judaize the promises of the Old Testament, ignoring the parts of the passages that indicate their solid grounding in Israelite faith and worship. Isaiah 58 is concerned not only with the poor and the hungry but also with fasting and the Sabbath, the latter listed alongside acts of social justice as preconditions for God's favor (Isa. 58:13–14). Indeed, sabbath observance offers foreigners and eunuchs entry into the community (Isa. 56:4–7). Similarly, Jesus's rejection by his hometown synagogue in Luke 4 does not erase the truth that the Gospels characterize his message as an expression of the values embedded in the texts and practices of his religious tradition. Christians too often tout the social justice aspects of the Prophets without recognizing their deep embeddedness within the Jewish tradition and talk about Jesus and justice without recognizing Judaism's commitment to justice. In the Prophets, the Gospels, and modern Judaism, ritual and ethics are deeply interwoven.

Reading Isaiah 2, 61, and 58 (along with Luke 4) apart from their literary and historical contexts allows activists to overlook the contextual specificities of justice in the past and in the present. These passages do not provide general moral principles but instead reflect the assumptions and aspirations of communities. But while these passages might not bear the weight of articulating a full and inclusive vision of justice, there is much in them that can enrich the work of activism. By taking seriously the literary and historical context of this rhetoric, we may find greater empathy with immigrant communities and more careful diagnosis of the causes of community polarization.

In a very real sense, the Judeans who relocated from Babylon to Jerusalem in the fifth century were immigrants. As descendants of those who had been forcibly deported in previous decades, their knowledge of this land had been mediated through the memories and hopes of their parents and grandparents. Their frustration and shock at the failure of the grand project of restoration, all within the context of Persian control, was the outcome of generational trauma and the distinct hopes it had generated. When the texts of Third Isaiah are read in this way, the voice of Isaiah 2, 58, and 61 sounds not like the courageous activist advocating for social justice but like the voice of those in countries trying to rebuild as foreign military forces withdraw, those whose images of a particular kind of future have been forged by empire.

A fruitful way of reading these texts is to focus on the pain that lies close under the surface of these words, attending not only to their complaints about the behavior of others (Isa. 59:9–11) but also the disillusionment with divine failure to act in ways that the ancestors remembered (Isa. 64:7–12). Such an approach frames the acrimony between groups in these texts as examples of "horizontal violence" or "lateral violence" transacted in the context of empire. As postcolonial theorists such as Homi Bhabha (Bhabha 2004) and Gayatri Spivak (Spivak 1988) have explained, those who have been oppressed and socialized as the colonized often turn against one another, mimicking the strategies of their oppressors in an act of internalized trauma.

Such a reading reminds me to analyze more thoughtfully the lateral violence and partisan polarization in my own country, recognizing not only the pain from which it grows but also the structures of power that have shaped our moral discourse. Much has been written about how the logic of exceptionalism and white supremacy has shaped the American psyche, how these "empires" have fed a moral rectitude that characterizes alternative points of view as not just wrong but evil. Indeed, a Pew survey reported in a 2022 edition of *The New Yorker* found that more than half of all Republicans and nearly half of all Democrats believe their political opponents to be "immoral" (Kolbert 2021). Perhaps fueling modern discourse is the legacy of our ancestors' desires: the mentality of European "settlers" denying legitimacy to the Indigenous populations, politics becoming a matter of domination rather than compromise.

CONCLUSION

Third Isaiah is certainly not alone in falling short of a full vision of justice for all people. Throughout history, almost every call for justice for one group intentionally or unintentionally has turned a blind eye toward justice for others. The American Revolution and the abolitionist movement both subordinated the fight for women's property and voting rights for other causes, the feminist movement of the 1960s did not address matters of race and class, and many today who fight discrimination against African Americans do not find common ground with activists for gay and lesbian causes.

In my experience, the primary way in which this myopia can be challenged is through connections—in person and through media—with people whose life experiences differ from our own. I have a profoundly different understanding of justice than I did twenty-five years ago, in part because I have had the privilege to teach and learn from diverse students, colleagues, and speakers from around the world. I have learned that while I can be an ally for LGBTQIA persons, I cannot speak for them; that my efforts to be a white anti-racist often unwittingly silence Black voices; that I too often overlook the divides of class and ableism. I am grateful, if sometimes wounded, by what I have learned when listening to others. As we seek to do greater justice, we need to listen more closely to those whom our own visions of justice disenfranchise.

8

The Individual Prophetic Voice

Jeremiah

While progressives love Amos and Micah for their *words* about justice, they love Jeremiah as a *person*. More than any other prophetic character, Jeremiah is envisioned as the embodiment of what it means to be a prophet: a courageous individual who stands in opposition to unjust leaders and institutions and who in retaliation faces scorn and suffering. Jeremiah is the role model for those who proclaim a scathing prophetic word that speaks truth to power.

Throughout the history of the progressive discourse that I explored in chapter 3, Jeremiah has been the hero. Following in the footsteps of Johann Herder and Robert Lowth, nineteenth-century biblical scholars cast Jeremiah in the Romantic mold: as a singular great man in conflict with those in power, particularly the priests. Heinrich Ewald's characterization of the prophet as the lonely reformer was expanded in the work of his students: Julius Wellhausen, who found in Jeremiah confirmation of his own valuation of individual spiritual experience over institutional religion, and Bernhard Duhm, whose extensive work on Jeremiah created a biography of Jeremiah which, according to Joseph Henderson, "follows the autobiography of Wordsworth, and . . . a similar story can be found in hundreds, if not thousands, of biographies, autobiographies, and novels in the century before Duhm's commentary" (Henderson 2019, 162).

In the twentieth century, Harry Emerson Fosdick approvingly cited Jeremiah's rejection of the sacrificial system and at Union Theological Seminary frequently taught courses on Jeremiah, declaring that "his was the richest experience of personal religion . . . known on earth before our Lord" (Miller 1985, 32). Max Weber, in his influential definition of "prophets" as charismatic rather than bureaucratic, named Jeremiah as the "purest and illustrates the prophet at the highest perfection"; according to his widow, Weber was fascinated with Jeremiah (Adair-Toteff 2014, 10).

In the present, Jeremiah continues to be emblematic of the scandalizing voice of unrelenting critique. In a 2017 article titled "The Prophetic Struggle of Kendrick Lamar's 'Damn,'" Rodney Carmichael calls Jeremiah Lamar's "patron saint": both employ rhetorical devices to express urgency, and their poetry unfolds in a "psychodrama" of protest and self-doubt (Carmichael 2017). Throughout all these portrayals, social activists become contemporary Jeremiahs.

This portrait of the prophet stands in some contrast to the church's historic characterization of Jeremiah as a harbinger of hope. Over the centuries, passages from Jeremiah have been read messianically, as pointing forward to the coming of Jesus. Such an understanding is implicit in the ways in which Jeremiah appears in the Revised Common Lectionary during the important liturgical seasons of Lent and Easter. The lectionary selects passages from Jeremiah's "Book of Consolation," a small section of the book brimming with promises for a new covenant (31:31–34) and a future Davidic king (33:14–16). These include

Jeremiah 31:1–6	Easter, year A
Jeremiah 31:7–14	Second Sunday after Christmas, years A, B, and C
Jeremiah 31:31–34	Fifth Sunday of Lent, year B
Jeremiah 33:14–16	First Sunday of Advent, year C

READING ALL OF JEREMIAH

Strikingly, neither of these characterizations does justice to the actual content of the book of Jeremiah or faces squarely its acerbic language and problematic theological claims. Jeremiah's words drip with violence and misogyny, and its dominant image of YHWH is as exacting deserved punishment. According to Jeremiah, the people's failure to worship YHWH alone provoked YHWH to send Nebuchadnezzar, king of the Babylonians, to destroy Judah. "By your own act you shall lose the heritage that I gave you" (17:4), YHWH claims in Jeremiah. "I myself will fight against you with outstretched hand and mighty arm, in anger, in fury, and in great wrath. And I will strike down the inhabitants of this city, both human beings and animals; they shall die of a great pestilence" (Jer. 21:5–6). Any resistance to the Babylonian armies is not only futile but unfaithful: "if any nation or kingdom will not serve this king, Nebuchadnezzar of Babylon, and put its neck under the yoke of the king of Babylon, then I will punish that nation with the sword, with famine, and with pestilence, says the LORD, until I have completed its destruction by his hand" (Jer. 27:8). While the lectionary does include multiple passages from Jeremiah in the semicontinuous Old Testament readings for year C (which I discuss shortly), none addresses squarely the depth and extent of Jeremiah's vitriol.

The progressive characterization of Jeremiah relies instead on selected aspects of the book. Most frequently cited are its compelling narratives that portray Jeremiah in conflict with leaders. The priest Pashur strikes the prophet and puts him in stocks (Jer. 20); when his unpopular speech continues, he is accosted by priests, prophets, and all the people and threatened with death (Jer. 26). He directly challenges the words of a rival prophet named Hananiah, whose death he foretells (Jer. 28). When his words are written on a scroll and read to the reigning monarch, the king cuts off each piece of the scroll as it is read and throws it in the fire (Jer. 36). Eventually, the king allows Jeremiah to be thrown into a waterless cistern to die (Jer. 38).

Also important to the progressive characterization are the "confessions" of the prophet, passages in which the prophet laments his own suffering and distress. More than in most other books, the prophet often seemingly speaks in his own name, as in Jeremiah 9:1, where a voice cries out,

> O that my head were a spring of water,
>   and my eyes a fountain of tears,
> so that I might weep day and night
>   for the slain of the daughter of my people!

Even though some scholars attribute the words to YHWH, most popular interpretations ascribe them to Jeremiah. The complaint in Jeremiah 20 is clearly that of the prophet, who protests that YHWH has enticed him, forcing him to say words that provoke others' violent response.

The focus on Jeremiah as a courageous individual is not without warrant. But it is a selective reading, and even more importantly, when we only read the book as the biography of a tortured prophet, we overlook key aspects of the book that invite deeper theological reflection for the activist.

REDACTION

Given the widespread progressive focus on Jeremiah as an individual, it is ironic that scholars have repeatedly and thoroughly demonstrated that the book itself is the product of extensive editing. It is not a simple transcript of a tortured activist but rather a complex literary compilation of diverse material.

There are many ways to recognize the book's complexity. Most apparent to even a casual reader, the material does not follow a logical chronological sequence. For example, the prophet's sermon in the Jerusalem Temple is recorded in Jeremiah 7, though its reception by the leaders of Jerusalem is not described until Jeremiah 26. The account of Jeremiah being beaten by Pashur appears in Jeremiah 20, though not until Jeremiah 36 is its consequence of banishment from the Temple explained. The casual reader likely also can recognize the dramatic shifts between the emotional poetic speeches cast in the first person and the more pious third-person narratives that are similar in outlook to the book of Deuteronomy (e.g., Jer. 18). While most of the prophetic books are marked by shifts in tone, Jeremiah stands out as particularly uneven. Carolyn Sharp speaks of the book's "irresolvable ideological tensions and awkward shifts of emphasis in the flow of material" (Sharp 2021, 29).

Other evidence of the book's editing, more evident to specialists in the field, includes the significant difference between the Hebrew text of Jeremiah on which most English translations are based (the medieval-era Masoretic Text) and the Greek version of the book on which earlier Roman Catholic Bibles were based (the ca. 200 BCE Septuagint). In the Septuagint, the book is one-eighth shorter, and a large chunk of material (the judgment against the nations) appears in a different location. While it would be easy to assume that the Septuagint simply shortened and rearranged the book, the situation is more complicated than that. A Hebrew manuscript of the short version of Jeremiah was found among the Dead Sea Scrolls, suggesting that the shorter book of Jeremiah was quite old. The longer version of the book, which we have today, likely was a later expansion of the Jeremiah tradition.

The historical context for this editorial activity was the aftermath of the destruction of Jerusalem by the neo-Babylonian armies. Scholars debate whether the final editing was completed under Babylonian rule and perhaps in Babylon itself (the exile) or after the repatriation of Judean descendants to Jerusalem under Persian rule (the postexilic period). In both scenarios, the catastrophe that the words anticipate had already taken place in the world of the audience.

As I explained in chapter 1, Jeremiah is not alone in this regard. Almost all of the Latter Prophets were likely edited after the exile to explain why Judah and Israel had fallen. They are theodicies, attempts to make sense of the unimaginable. What makes Jeremiah so striking is not the fact that it reflects the trauma of Jerusalem's destruction but instead the way it deals with this trauma by giving it the face of an *individual*.

The editorial expansion of the Masoretic Text (MT) accentuated the characterization of Jeremiah as an individual. While in the shorter version the speaker of the Confessions is more generic, akin to laments from the Psalms, the longer MT version explicitly frames the words as those of Jeremiah, who like Job laments his individual fate (Diamond 1990, 37). In the MT, the events of Jeremiah's life "all take on paradigmatic force. In the end, Jeremiah emerges as YHWH's suffering servant, not unlike Second Isaiah's 'servant of the LORD,' enduring enormous hardship at the hands of his enemies" (Stulman 2018, 1070). The individualization of Jeremiah is not a historical record of his distinctive individuality but a characterization carefully crafted by editors: not a person but a persona.

That individualization was further extended in the later reuses of the Jeremiah tradition. Already in the postexilic 2 Chronicles 35:25, Jeremiah was known as one who laments, a characterization that expanded to Jeremiah being named in the Septuagint, the Dead Sea Scrolls, and later Jewish and Christian literature as the author of the book of Lamentations. Once Jeremiah was imagined as the author of Lamentations, his reputation as the lonely voice overlooking destruction was further cemented in the interpretive imagination. Rembrandt's 1630 painting of an elderly Jeremiah looking forlornly away from a burning Jerusalem captures this sense of his isolation.

Through its editorial process, the MT molded the prophet Jeremiah into an archetype of the tortured outsider. But the purpose of this individualization, as I explore, was not for the sake of the individual but of the community.

JEREMIAH AS THE PRODUCT OF A TRAUMATIZED COMMUNITY

One of the most fruitful developments in biblical interpretation in the past few decades has been the engagement of trauma studies. Building on the insights of psychologists such as Judith Herman (Herman 1997) and Bessel van der Kolk (van der Kolk 2014) as well as its application to texts by literary critics such as Cathy Caruth (Caruth 1996), trauma-informed biblical studies has explored the complex ways in which these texts reflect, hide, deflect, relive, and reframe the deep physical, emotional, and psychic suffering of individuals and communities.

Describing the experiences of ancient Judeans during the sixth century BCE (and beyond) as "the fall of Jerusalem" can obscure the brutal realities of these events. When in the sixth century BCE the southern kingdom revolted against decades of Babylonian control, the empire's armies besieged the city of Jerusalem and eventually breached its protective walls. Judeans would have experienced starvation, sexual assault, and the deaths of young and old—and witnessed the maiming of their king and the execution of officials, the desecration of the Temple, the destruction of the city, the forced deportation of survivors to a foreign land, and the shattering of a theology that trusted that YHWH would protect the nation, its Temple, and its Davidic king. The trauma would have been both profoundly personal and profoundly social, economic, and theological.

Although readers of the Bible often describe the community formed in Jerusalem in the fifth century under Persian control as the end of the Judeans' suffering, calling it "the restoration," "the return," or "the postexilic period," the Judeans' earlier trauma was both extended and augmented in this period. Those who relocated from Babylon to Jerusalem were not the original survivors of the Babylonian deportation but their descendants—yet they continued to describe themselves as "the exile" and tell the stories of destruction as their own. The trauma of their parents and grandparents had been "socially mediated" (Alexander 2004), passed down as their identity. Living in the Persian province of Yehud after this repatriation was not a matter of restoration and freedom but, as I explained in chapter 7, one of navigating the external and internal dynamics of the Persian occupation.

The dynamics of trauma permeate the book of Jeremiah, giving shape to its language. As Kathleen O'Connor has masterfully shown, the book processes the catastrophe indirectly, "slant," using metaphor and imagery that echoes the violence but reframes it (O'Connor 2010, 2011). For example, behind the image of a Daughter Zion fainting and gasping for breath before killers (Jer. 4:31), O'Connor discerns the memory of human women facing invading armies; and behind the scandalous claim that YHWH will sexually humiliate Jerusalem (Jer. 13:26–27), she hears the devastating truth of wartime rape. She hears underneath Jeremiah's language the same starvation, death, and despair described more explicitly in Lamentations 2 and Psalm 79.

The book's theological claims about divine violence and punishment as deserved are problematic on many levels. The history of Christian interpretation underscores their dangerous potential for feeding anti-Judaism. Reading these passages at face value offers proof that YHWH destroyed ancient Israel and Judah because of their disobedience and now only honors the "new covenant" offered to believers through Jesus. In such an interpretation, Christians embrace the hope offered by the Prophets as their own, while applying their message of punishment to others. This is a risk faced by those who only preach from Jeremiah according to the Revised Common Lectionary assignments for Lent, Easter, and Advent, which draw exclusively from the hopeful "Book of Consolation" in liturgical seasons that invite reflection on the messiahship of Jesus.

These biblical passages also are too easily invoked to insist that all tragedies are the result of God's punishment. Even though these texts never claim that all suffering comes from God, they are often applied in a way that blames victims for their own suffering—that a natural disaster was caused by a city's openness to diverse people, that a national defeat was inevitable because people failed to follow God's laws, or that individuals' suffering resulted from their moral failings. Such a theology can be devastating to victims of physical and emotional violence, who receive and internalize misplaced blame while powerful people and powerful systems remain unchecked.

O'Connor does not deny these problems, nor does she believe that the book of Jeremiah offers an eternal word for navigating trauma. But she does suggest that reading Jeremiah through trauma-informed lenses offers a way of recognizing how this explanation of Judah's fall serves to make the devastation intelligible and, in a seemingly counterintuitive way, gives agency to survivors. If there is a reason for what happened and we have a role to play, then our future actions can influence future outcomes. Her claim is that Jeremiah's theology does not stand the test of enduring doctrine but that, for survivors, "It keeps God from disappearing through a temporary stay against confusion" (O'Connor 2011, 137).

In a different context, the psychologist and Holocaust survivor Viktor Frankl discussed how such meaning-making benefits individuals. Himself imprisoned in a Nazi concentration camp, he observed that those who bestowed meaning and purpose on their horrific experiences had the greatest rates of survival (Frankl 1985). Other authors also have underscored the ways in which communities make meaning after disaster, how reframing cultural memories for the purposes of the present allows the group to find continuity with its past and hope for its future. This kind of meaning-making runs through the Deuteronomistic History and the Latter Prophets, allowing the community to see YHWH as noncapricious, fair, and ultimately available—and to see their own actions as important and productive.

The book of Jeremiah (at least the MT version) is so distinctive because it makes an individual the embodiment of the community's response to trauma. The prophet representatively voices the punishment as deserved (adopting the posture that the community is instructed to take) and also laments the suffering it exacts upon his body and emotional health (reflecting the community's own experience). Such accusation and lament are reflected in Jeremiah 4:19–22 (discussed below), in which the prophet cries out, "My anguish, my anguish!" at hearing the sounds of war and laments that "disaster overtakes disaster," before turning to blame the people for its cause. Elsewhere in Jeremiah 4 and in the book, lament becomes actual protest against YHWH, who is accused of deceiving the people (Jer. 4:10) and the prophet (Jer. 20:7). Through the persona of Jeremiah, the community is both taught the book's theological claim and also allowed to lament and protest the message as well.

WHAT TO MAKE OF JEREMIAH?

To interpret the book of Jeremiah representatively, honestly and clearly,
requires engaging more of its content than selected verses of messianic promise or images of Jeremiah in conflict with leaders. One key opportunity to
do so is offered by The Revised Common Lectionary's semi-continuous First
Readings in the Season after Pentecost in Year C. This sequence is focused on
the prophetic books and includes eight passages from Jeremiah:

1:4–10	Jeremiah's commission; Proper 16, year C
2:4–13	The people are accused of idolatry; Proper 17, year C
18:1–11	Jeremiah visits the potter's house; Proper 18, year C
4:11–12, 22–28	Words of judgment; Proper 19, year C
8:18–9:1	Lament over the fate of the nation; Proper 20, year C
32:1–3a, 6–15	While imprisoned, Jeremiah commissions the buying of family land; Proper 21, year C
29:1, 4–7	Advice for the exiles to settle in Babylon: Proper 23, year C
31:27–34	YHWH promises to rebuild Judah and create a new covenant; Proper 24, year C

When read in a continuous sequence, these passages incorporate many of
Jeremiah's insistent themes. They include blame on the nation for its sins,
decrees of punishment, lament, the individualization of the prophetic figure,
and an ending note of hope.

Yet this list omits many of the details of Jeremiah's claims. There is little
of the explicit naming of the Babylonians as YHWH's tool of destruction as
can be found in Jeremiah 25:8–10 and Jeremiah 21:3–7; instead, the words
of judgment in Jeremiah 4:11–12, 22–28 speak vaguely of "a hot wind" that
comes against the people. The early verses of Jeremiah 32:1–3a, 6–15 do set
Jeremiah's confinement in the context of Nebuchadnezzar's siege of Jerusalem, but omitted are verses 3b–5, which directly state that YHWH hand
Jerusalem over to the Babylonians. Missing from this list also is Jeremiah's
insistence on submission to Babylon, as expressed in Jeremiah 27:1–11.

In four of the eight lections, the prophet Jeremiah plays a significant role.
His commissioning in Jeremiah 1:4–10 invites us to imagine him as a youth,
and the narratives of the potter's house (Jer. 18:1–11) and his buying land
while imprisoned (Jer. 32:1–3a, 6–15) focus on how he acts in response to
divine directive. The voice of lament in Jeremiah 8:18–9:1 has been variously
identified by scholars but is easily interpreted as the voice of Jeremiah, the
"weeping prophet."

The verses selected in Jeremiah 4:11–12, 22–28 omit both significant lament and actual protest of YHWH's actions. As noted earlier, in verse 10, the prophet accuses YHWH of having deceived the people. Jeremiah 4:19–21 expresses intense emotional distress ("My anguish!" "I writhe in pain," 4:19), the reality of the devastation ("Disaster overtakes disaster," 4:20), and complaint ("How long?" 4:21). The lectionary has downplayed the depth of the despair, the book's focus on the Babylonians, and the voice of protest, while playing up the image of Jeremiah as an individual and, of course, by creating a trajectory of readings that culminates with hope. Yet reading these passages systematically over the course of multiple weeks allows hearers to experience the pain and brutality of the book of Jeremiah.

In my teaching and personal experience, interpreting such texts through the lens of trauma theory has multiple advantages. First, calling attention to the historical and existential situation faced by the first audience of this text allows hearers to have greater empathy with the plight of ancient Judeans, to recognize that easy theological claims that "they were punished for their sins" overlooks the deep suffering of our ancestors of faith. Second, that empathy for the past can extend into willingness to consider the realities of communal trauma in the present. National tragedies such as the September 11 attacks, the devastation of the COVID pandemic, and the political acrimony that followed in their wakes become contemporary parallels. Focusing on the trauma underneath Jeremiah also opens us to considering traumas facing local communities, such as floodings, wildfire, gun violence, and racialized killings. Trauma-informed readings invite nations, towns, and even individual congregations to name the assaults on their own communal life. They can increase empathy for those in the past and present who experience invasion and gain greater appreciation for the ability of those who are suffering to stay in relationship with God.

The third advantage of reading Jeremiah as a trauma response has mixed results. Recognizing the contingent nature of Jeremiah's theological explanation of the community's suffering, seeing it as the "temporary stay against confusion" that O'Connor describes, can help us resist attempts to universalize Jeremiah's claim that Judah was destroyed by God because of its own sin. If this, in Frankl's words, is an act of meaning-making shaped by the circumstances, then it need not be understood as a description of how God always behaves; it challenges confidence in the ability to connect the dots between suffering and sin. That is, such an approach allows hearers to ask the same questions as Jeremiah but seek answers more appropriate to their own contexts. How does a nation, a town, or even an individual congregation make sense of the devastations they are experiencing? Where is God in the midst of painful communal realities?

Yet this approach leaves little for those seeking a more enduring, life-giving image of God. If it is a "temporary stay against confusion," it offers little for the long haul. A trauma-informed reading of Jeremiah does not solve all of the challenges of reading this book. It can serve to "excuse" all of Jeremiah's problems as "just" the reflections of trauma. Its misogyny, its political stances, and its characterization of a violent God can be downplayed for the sake of empathy with the ancient traumatized community. In her powerful commentary, Carolyn Sharp resists such an apology for Jeremiah (Sharp 2022). She instead critiques the ways in which the persona of Jeremiah was co-opted by the book's authors, who maintained that those deported to Babylon were superior to those left behind. She delves deeply into the implications of its gender constructions for women, gay, and trans folk.

As I have learned over a long career of teaching and preaching, interpretive frameworks often fail to resolve the visceral reactions that folks have to disturbing biblical texts. I encountered this reality while leading a workshop on Jeremiah for pastors preparing for the upcoming lectionary season. As we systematically worked through these eight Jeremiah passages, preachers became increasingly disturbed. Words of judgment and wrath could be absorbed while reading two or three passages, but the relentless volley of judgment soon wore them down—and they protested. "I thought the prophets were supposed to be on the side of justice," they insisted. "How is this justice?" "If Jeremiah is so insistent on YHWH's anger and punishment, how can I preach that message repeatedly and still offer good news?" Actually *reading* Jeremiah felt violent to their spirits. I also have witnessed generations of students experience the same shock, discomfort, and disorientation that the pastors in the lectionary workshop reported, and while they can intellectually explain alternative frameworks for thinking about the material, they still feel its assault.

Yet I have also heard powerful testimonies to the healing that engaging Jeremiah in a sensitive and thoughtful context can offer. While speaking about Jeremiah and trauma in an adult class in a progressive congregation, I met Meara, who later shared with me her story of taking a seminary course on Jeremiah less than two months after having been sexually assaulted. From the very beginning of her seminar, she was taught to critique—and how to critique—the violence of Jeremiah's rhetoric; she was assigned the work of feminist and womanist scholars who helped her know, from the outset, that abuse was not okay and must be critiqued. Her wise instructor also designed the course in ways that allowed participants to talk about their own experiences in the midst of a supportive community, so that engaging Jeremiah became not only an analytical exercise but also a profoundly interactive and human one.

Because she was prepared to read Jeremiah's rhetoric and equipped to critique its harm, she was able to interact with the book in ways that she found life-giving and hopeful. She found most helpful the images in Jeremiah 9 of weeping women, called by God to lead the community through its grief. The permission to lament, modeled by this book and its eponymous prophet, opened her to her own process of grief. Meara shared that these images from Jeremiah have stayed with her over time, providing resources throughout her life. When years later she experienced the death of her husband, she found that the image of a weeping God helped her to feel, as she had after the assault, that God was with her in her pain. For Meara, knowing how to resist the toxic aspects of Jeremiah gave her the freedom to find healing in its words.

JEREMIAH AND ITS READERS

In this chapter I've argued that the emphasis given by progressives on the heroic individuality of the prophet Jeremiah has some grounding in the book itself but has been exaggerated at the expense of other aspects of the book. In contrast, contemporary scholars are increasingly interpreting the book as the product of a community processing social and cultural trauma, while raising hard questions about the book's theology and rhetoric.

Both the individualist and the trauma-based interpretations are reflections of the social contexts of their interpreters. Here and more extensively in chapter 3, I've pointed to the ways that the values of the Enlightenment, Romanticism, and the Social Gospel, fused with "scientific" biblical scholars, helped cast all prophets (and especially Jeremiah) as countercultural voices who resist those in power at the expense of their own well-being. For modern progressives, such sensibilities are amplified by cultural factors such as a suspicion of those in power and the belief in the power of the individual voice to serve as a whistleblower.

The current attention being given to trauma theory, not only in biblical studies but also in education, public health, and psychology, is also a reflection of its time. It should not surprise us when modern scholars describe ancient Judah in ways that look much like the present: communities traumatized by forced deportation and military conflict, reeling from change and disillusionment, bombarded by arguments about what founding documents really mean, and what approach to the future offers any hope for survival. No less than scholars of the past, contemporary views of the Prophets are a reflection of human ideological, theological, and philosophical assumptions and other interpretations of what is going on in the world.

I am convinced that when we bring awareness of all these dimensions of our interpretation to our interpretation of Jeremiah—informed of the history of interpretation that has shaped us, conscious of our own cultural context, thoroughly grounded in the details of the literature itself, and equipped to resist a simple acceptance of its problematic ideologies—we can, like Meara, find that the book might speak a word to our own hurting hearts and to a traumatized world.

9

The Prophets and Ecological Justice

Second Isaiah

In the past several decades, faith-based social justice movements have expanded to address the environmental catastrophe facing our planet and its diverse inhabitants. Advocacy against structural racism and economic disparity has been joined with activism on behalf of Earth.

The crisis of Earth is indeed dire. The rapidly accelerating devastation of all components of our ecosystem is ubiquitously evident not only in the scientific information drawn from natural sources such as ice cores, rocks, and tree rings, but also in the easily observed realities of increasingly severe wildfires, drought, flooding, sea-level rise, and pollution.

Human activity is the indisputable cause of this devastation. As reported by NASA, 97 percent of actively publishing climate scientists agree that global warming and climate change are being caused by humans (NASA n.d.). According to the March 2023 report of the Intergovernmental Panel on Climate Change,

> Human activities, principally through emissions of greenhouse gases, have unequivocally caused global warming, with global surface temperature reaching 1.1°C above 1850–1900 in 2011–2020. Global greenhouse gas emissions have continued to increase, with unequal historical and ongoing contributions arising from unsustainable energy use, land use and land-use change, lifestyles and patterns of consumption and production across regions, between and within countries, and among individuals. (IPCC 2023)

Tellingly, our era is now being called the Anthropocene, or "age of the human," due to the damaging mark that human activity is leaving in the geological record.

Also manifestly evident is the reality that not all humans share the blame for and burden of these planetary changes. Health outcomes for Black and white communities in the United States and around the globe are highly inequitable: Black children in both the United States and Great Britain are more likely than whites to be exposed to air pollution, lead poisoning, and other toxins, even when their families earn comparable incomes (World Economic Forum 2020). Similar analysis is emerging for the role that gendered, racialized, and colonialized sensibilities play in driving ecological imperialism. Many environmental activists are targeting "environmental racism," a term first used in 1982 by the Reverend Dr. Ben Chavis while protesting the dumping of forty thousand cubic yards of toxic soil in a poor Black community of Warren County, North Carolina.

Particularly among religious progressives who accept the legitimacy of scientific findings, voluntary associations, denominations, and interfaith coalitions are calling for climate action. Jewish, Sikh, Unitarian Universalist, and Islamic movements run alongside and often in cooperation with organizations such as Interfaith Power and Light, the Evangelical Climate Initiative, Green Faith, and denominational initiatives such as Presbyterians for Earth Care (PCUSA) and the "Creation Care" of the Episcopal Church. The United Church of Christ invites congregations to "Become a Creation Justice Church," and Creation Justice Ministries includes thirty-eight national faith bodies including the United States Conference of Catholic Bishops, the National Council of Churches of Christ, and the Jewish Council for Public Affairs. In these and other efforts, justice extends beyond economic equity to recognize the interconnectedness of and danger threatening all life.

THE CREATION PARADIGM

As reflected in the names of many of these campaigns, the dominant paradigm for Christian faith-based climate advocacy is grounded in the Bible's stories and poems about creation. The key text, of course, is Genesis 1–2, which environmentalists read as a celebration of Earth's beauty and God-endowed goodness, as well as the articulation of the responsibility of humans to be good stewards of its bounty. Other verses inform the creation paradigm as well: psalms that celebrate the natural world and the animal kingdom (Pss. 19; 24, 104); YHWH's speech in the book of Job, which catalogues, like a *National Geographic* special, the amazing characteristics of nonhuman creatures (Job 38–39); and Jesus' reminder that God cares about the birds of the air and the lilies of the field (Matt. 6:28). From the prophetic books, most commonly cited are passages from Second Isaiah (Isa. 40–55) that characterize YHWH as the sole Creator of and authority over all things.

In this advocacy paradigm, care for Earth is not only a scientific matter but a theological and biblically based mandate. Earth is not merely a planet but God's creation. Responsibility for its health is not merely a matter of self-interest or self-importance, but it is a divine requirement that humans engage in "creation care" or "creation stewardship." Such is the conviction of Pope Francis, who in his encyclical *Laudato Si'* insists that

> faith convictions can offer Christians, and some other believers as well, ample motivation to care for nature and for the most vulnerable of their brothers and sisters. If the simple fact of being human moves people to care for the environment of which they are a part, Christians in their turn "realize that their responsibility within creation, and their duty towards nature and the Creator, are an essential part of their faith." (Francis 2015, 2.1, with quotes from Pope John Paul II)

In turn, "stewardship" is the primary lens through which many Christians read the Bible ecologically. Drawing on the imperative for humans to till the garden in Genesis 2:15, "keeping the garden of God becomes a vocation of dignity and partnership for the thriving of all life, human and other-than-human" (Brunner and Swoboda 2022, 417).

The advantages of a faith-based paradigm for environmental activism are clear. It not only grants biblical precedent and authority to environmental concerns but also provides a counterpoint to contrary Christian perspectives. Christians with millennialist and apocalyptic theological leanings, for example, commonly deny that the climate is changing or that humans are to blame for climate change. If the church is soon to be raptured and if Jesus predicted that cataclysmic weather will mark his return (Mark 13:28; Luke 21:11), then the appropriate preparation is not mitigating Earth's crisis but preparing one's soul to meet Jesus. In a 2021 Facebook post, evangelist Franklin Graham took precisely this position, ridiculing the G20 Summit focus on climate change and asserting, "I believe we are one minute to midnight—not regarding climate change, but on God's clock, when he will bring judgment on those who have rejected him and his Son, Jesus Christ." A creation paradigm for climate advocacy provides an important counternarrative to such views, fascinatingly by turning to the Old Testament to challenge particular readings of the New Testament.

Yet for all of its value, the creation paradigm for Christian climate activism is woefully inadequate for the current crisis. Given that we are far past climate change and instead are facing climate catastrophe, the situation before us is no longer one of diagnosis and simplistic responses. In the words of Fred Simmons, we are called not to alarm but autopsy; or, speaking from Simmons's Christian Augustinian/Lutheran perspective, it is time to face the death that is the consequence of sin (Simmons 2019). In a similar vein, Tim Beal seeks a palliative approach to the human future, accepting the reality of humanity's finitude (Beal 2022).

The framework of "care" and "stewardship" implies that the world is as beautiful and wondrous as it was created to be and that humans are called to the task of maintenance and the prevention of harm. Yet the Earth is not now as God created it. Humans have already wrecked the planet and have been doing so for a long time. Scientists debate about when the "inadvertent climate vandalism" of the Anthropocene Era began—during the Industrial Revolution, when factories began mass emissions of carbon, or during the Agricultural Revolution, when humans began to permanently alter the landscape for our benefit by burning trees, destroying the soil, and domesticating the cattle that are now the dominant species on Earth (Grinspoon 2016, 158). Yet all agree that the devastation is extensive and accelerating rapidly. Earth's alarms are not calling for management of a good creation but of an emergency response to crisis.

For this reason, Christian theologians are critiquing inherited Christologies, soteriologies, and environmental tropes such as "stewardship" that are well-meaning but ultimately ignore the Earth as it is now (Deane-Drummond, Bergmann, and Vogt 2017). The Exeter Project, a research cooperative directed by David Horrell at the University of Exeter, critiques the common model of "stewardship" on many levels:

- It gives humanity a "managerial" role—as if they were "left in charge" by an absentee landlord. Does this mean God has disappeared from the scene?
- It regards the world as a "natural resource," to be managed well for human benefit. Or it may suggest that nature is best when "managed" by humans—organising "wilderness" into "garden."
- It is an arrogant ethic, suggesting that humans have both the right and the ability to organise creation, and that nature is better off when managed by us. It is highly anthropocentric (human-centred), putting humans in a unique and privileged position. (Exeter Project n.d.)

Along with the Exeter Project, multiple philosophers and theologians have insisted that at the root of the environmental crisis is anthropocentrism and a belief in human exceptionalism. When humans believe that their comfort, safety, and perceived needs take precedence over all other considerations, that they are the pinnacle of creation and therefore that creation is for their benefit, then Earth becomes a reservoir from which resources for human consumption can be extracted. Progressives are not exempt from such views, given the deep connection between progressive thought, Enlightenment rationalism, and the logic of white supremacy. The description of this ideology by Willie Jennings that I included in chapter 4 is worth repeating here: it is the idolatry of "white self-sufficient masculinity" in which the educated man manages himself, commands all knowledge, and ultimately seeks to master not only others but also the world (Jennings 2020, 18, 31).

Deeper analyses insist that "anthropocentrism" itself is a false ideology that obscures the deep inequalities between humans behind a veil of a supposed universal human trait. Joerg Rieger's *Theology in the Capitalocene* drives this point home. The crisis facing the Earth and human well-being, he argues, is driven not by all humans but by a capitalistic system in which "the economic interests of a small and privileged group of humans rule both people and the planet" (Rieger 2022, 2). "Not all of humanity, and not even the majority of humanity, is driving the exploitation of the nonhuman environment and benefiting from it—just like the majority of humanity is hardly benefiting from the exploitation of human labor or from the largely uncontrolled CO_2 emissions produced by neoliberal capitalism" (Rieger 2022, 29). Blaming everyone for consumerism, for example, overlooks the imperative for generating wealth by those who produce goods and drive their marketing.

Rieger's claims rely heavily on the work of ecofeminists, eco-womanists, and those who approach ecology though a postcolonial lens. Challenging the easy trope that climate catastrophe is the exclusive concern of developed, "educated" countries, explorations of environmental racism underscore that the stratification of wealth and the exploitation of vulnerable people go hand in hand with abuse of Earth. The labor of the enslaved or undercompensated and the unpaid reproductive and domestic work of women are closely linked with the assumption that Earth provides "free" resources for wealth production.

These critiques underscore that, for all of the appeal of "creation care" and "creation stewardship," Christian climate activism must move beyond these models. Even when we celebrate creation and talk about our responsibility for creation care, we too often do so in a way that focuses on humans as the pinnacle of God's purposes and allows us to think about Earth as a garden to leisurely tend rather than a planet already, perhaps irrevocably, changed by our selfishness. Rather than simply repeat biblical passages that praise nature, effective activism must take seriously the extent of Earth's devastation and the dynamics of power between humans that fuels it. It must be willing to engage in critique not only of society but also, if necessary, of the ideology embedded in the biblical texts themselves. We must be brutally honest about our "creation" texts, to see their limitations and even the damage they have done.

Then and only then can we consider other ways that these texts might fuel our ecological activism.

CREATION IN GENESIS 1–2

Before turning to the creation texts in the Prophets, I consider first the creation narratives in Genesis 1–2. Because these chapters are the foundation upon which the creation care paradigm rests, a consideration of the logic inherent in them is important.

Genesis 1 describes the deity (here called Elohim, "God") as systematically creating everything in the heavens and on the Earth in six days, calling it all "good." In one last act before resting on the Sabbath, Elohim creates humans in the divine image and commands that they be fruitful and multiply, and then "have dominion" over all other creatures (Gen. 1:26, 28) and "subdue" the earth (Gen. 1:28). A second creation narrative in Genesis 2:4a–3:24 depicts YHWH (the name of the deity having shifted) as forming the first human from dust and placing him in the garden to "till it and keep it" (Gen. 2:15) before making the second human. When both disobey YHWH's command, they are punished with the demands of agricultural labor and with mortality (Gen. 3:17–19).

In 1967 the historian Lynn White issued a direct critique of the creation narrative, insisting that its anthropocentrism is not only toxic but also to blame for the West's utilitarian attitudes for nature: it is the problem of the environmental crisis rather than its solution. According to White, Genesis "not only established a dualism of man and nature but also insisted that it is God's will that man exploit nature for his proper ends" (White 1967, 1205). He linked the logics of technology and colonialism, arguing, "Both our present science and our present technology are so tinctured with orthodox Christian arrogance toward nature that no solution for our ecological crisis can be expected from them alone" (White 1967, 1205–6).

In response to White's critique, ecologically minded Christians have tried to redeem these texts. I have met diverse Christians who, without knowing any Hebrew, explain to me that the terms "subdue" and "dominion" are softer than they sound; because we are to act like God and because God loves creation, surely we too must love creation. In *Laudato Si'*, Pope Francis similarly downplayed the weight of these terms, explaining that the directive to "till" in Genesis 2:15 provides the contextual framework for understanding "dominion" in Genesis 1:28 as caretaking (Francis 2015, 1.66).

While Genesis 1–2 cannot be blamed for all environmental devastation, White's claim that Genesis 1–2 assumes and supports the interests of humans remains valid. The relevant verbs in Genesis 1:28 are not gentle ones. The

Hebrew word translated as "subdue" also is used in Jeremiah 34:11 for the "subjection" of slaves. The Hebrew for "have dominion" appears in Leviticus 26:17 in the context of foes "rul[ing]" over the conquered, and Psalm 72:8 expresses the desire that the Davidic king will "have dominion" over all the earth. The argument from canonical context, such as Pope Francis employs, can work in various ways, depending on which verses are chosen to interpret others. For example, in Joshua 11, the conquering Israelites are commanded to hamstring horses and burn towns (Josh. 11:6, 13) rather than respect animals and air quality.

Creation care ethics casts Genesis 1:1–24a universally as an account of the beginning of all people and all things and as the guidelines for all humanity. A careful reading of this chapter instead reveals that it is firmly grounded in the identity of a particular people. The pinnacle of creation in Genesis 2:2 is not the creation of humans but of the Sabbath, a distinctively Jewish religious observance. The categorization of animals "according to their kinds" in Genesis 1:20–25 serves not to mark an orderly creation but as the framework for the taxonomy of kosher and nonkosher foods in the book of Leviticus. Written by the same Priestly authors as Genesis 1, Leviticus explains that animals that swarm on the earth (Lev. 11:41) rather than creep on the earth (Gen. 1:24) are "detestable" because they fail to behave according to their "kind." In Genesis and Leviticus, the order of creation undergirds the identity markers of the author's community. While Ellen Davis has discerned within Leviticus a valuable environmental ethic (Davis 2009), it is also true that Leviticus seeks to craft a community identity over and against others, whom it calls "Canaanites."

A thoughtful exploration of Genesis 2–3 similarly challenges the assumption that it advances a wholesome environmental ethic. The task of tilling and caring for the garden is not one given for the sake of all creatures but for the sake of what the humans might eat. Written by a different author than the previous story, this narrative underscores the differences between humans and animals (Gen. 2:20), the social structures in which humans partner (Gen. 2:24), and the vicissitudes of agricultural life (Gen. 3:17–19).

Read in its literary and historical contexts, then, Genesis 1–3 is less about everyone and everything than about the identity of their authors' community. Like other biblical texts, they "do not directly address modern epistemology, concerns, and/or questions on any number of topics, including the ecocrisis" (Leese 2019, 4).

SECOND ISAIAH'S CREATION THEOLOGY

Isaiah 40–55, also known as Deutero-Isaiah, is much beloved within progressive thought. In the nineteenth century, this anonymous prophet was heralded as advancing Israelite thought toward the sublime truths of universalism and pure monotheism. Wellhausen credited "Isaiah of the exile" with praising God "as the author of the world and of all nature" such that "Israel is in exclusive possession of the universal truth, which cannot perish with Israel, but must, through the instrumentality of Israel, become the common possession of the whole world" (Wellhausen [1881] 1973, 417). According to Abraham Kuenen, this "ethical monotheism," in which the existence of only one God meant that there was only one universal morality, was the creation of the prophets but was completed with Jesus (Kuenen 1877, 585, 589, 592). In protest against these Christian appropriations, the Jewish philosopher Hermann Cohen maintained that the moral codes of the God of Israel, as expressed by the prophets, were universal moral codes for all; he credited Judaism, not Christianity, with its highest expression: "To assert that there is only one God for all of humanity is thus to assert a universal ethical ideal, one on which individuals see all people as 'fellow humans,' and not as 'others' who can be excluded from the moral community" (Edgar 2021). Despite this demur, in the early twentieth century Harry Emerson Fosdick likewise described Jesus as following in a line of prophets that included Second Isaiah by linking morality—which for Fosdick was synonymous with social justice—with belief in a single God (Fosdick 1938, 40).

In the twentieth century, the trend of attributing philosophical monotheism and high ethical ideals to Second Isaiah continued, but greater attention turned to its characterization of God as Earth's sole *creator*. While for most of his career the German theologian Gerhard von Rad described "creation theology" as a late (an inferior) addendum to the Israelite creed that God had acted in history, he nonetheless credited Second Isaiah with not only introducing a focus on creation but also linking creation with God's great acts of salvation (von Rad 1965, 240–41).

In the twenty-first century, greater attention is being paid to the ecological dimensions of Second Isaiah's articulation of YHWH as the sole Creator of the world. In his powerful work of ecological advocacy, *Seven Pillars of Creation*, William Brown celebrates Second Isaiah for describing God not only as the original Creator but as an ongoing one, one who is creating a new thing: its vision parallels that of modern science, in which the Earth continually engages in convergence and symbiosis (Brown 2010, 218–20). On a more popular level, Isaiah 40 and 43 regularly appear in internet lists of biblical passages calling for care of creation, including on denominational websites (Watkins 2021).

Second Isaiah does describe YHWH as Creator more than other parts of the Bible. The Hebrew verb for "create" (*bara*) and its related forms describe YHWH as the Creator of all things (Isa. 40:26, 20, 28; 41:5; 45:7, 8, 12, 18; 54:16); the creator of Israel/Jacob (Isa. 43:1, 7, 15); and the creator of plans for Israel's redemption (Isa. 48:7). More than most other biblical collections, it pointedly insists that Israel's deity cannot be compared to other gods: YHWH alone created the sea and the heavens, while other gods are mere idols (Isa. 40:12–26) made of wood and metal (Isa. 44:9–20). The Revised Common Lectionary includes several of these texts:

Isaiah 40:21–31   Fifth Sunday after Epiphany, year B
Isaiah 45:1–7   Proper 24, year A

And yet when read in the literary context of this collection, these claims of YHWH's singularity do not espouse a general philosophical or theological principle about creation theology but instead serve a particular function with Second Isaiah's rhetorical argument. The summation of that argument is stated most clearly in Isaiah 48:20:

> Go out from Babylon, flee from Chaldea;
>   declare this with a shout of joy, proclaim it,
> send it forth to the end of the earth;
>   say, "The LORD has redeemed his servant Jacob!"

Isaiah 40–54 addresses the descendants of Judeans who had been forcibly deported to Babylon in the sixth century BCE, cajoling them to leave Babylon and relocate to Jerusalem. All of the arguments of Second Isaiah are constructed to support this appeal to return. *Because* YHWH is the Creator of all things and more powerful than the idols of Babylonian religion, those returning will face no obstacles to their return. *Because* Yahweh has forgiven Jerusalem, loves the people, and is ready to comfort them, they can trust in the divine plan (Isa. 40–47). Indeed, YHWH has anointed Cyrus, the ruler of the Persian Empire, to tear down the doors of Babylon so that they may return home (Isa. 45). Israel, once the suffering servant, will soon be vindicated (Isa. 52–53), and Daughter Zion the bereft mother will soon witness the homecoming of her children (Isa. 49; 54). These and other arguments are mounted to convince the second and third generations of Judeans living in Babylon to engage in "reverse migration." To be willing to relocate to a place that they had never lived, they would need to be convinced that they belonged in Jerusalem, that the Babylonian gods were inferior, and that YHWH would ease the rigors of travel. Their pathos for Jerusalem—the mother grieving her lost children—would need to be stirred, and their identity as the servant of YHWH would need to be solidified. As in the case of modern migrant communities, the "myth of homeland" would need to be created.

Recognizing this literary and historical context underscores that Second Isaiah's claims about YHWH are not philosophical truths but pragmatic arguments about the superiority of Judah's god over the gods of Babylon. Indeed, many of the claims seem to be a direct refutation of Babylonian beliefs that the god Marduk controlled the "tablet of the destinies": "World creation (or rather world design) and determination of destiny are two sides of the same coin" (Albani 2020, 229). These claims are less about a creation theology and monotheism than about YHWH's power to authorize and facilitate repatriation. The linking of creation and the orchestration of history is made explicit in Isaiah 45:12–13:

> I made the earth
>   and created humankind upon it. . . .
> I have aroused Cyrus in righteousness,
>   and I will make all of his paths straight.

Yahweh is also actively *altering* Earth for the sake of this plan, leveling mountains and in-filling valleys (Isa. 40)—not simply an original Creator but also an active geological engineer. YHWH transplants evergreens outside of their natural ecosystem into the desert (Isa. 41:18–20) and provides for their irrigation. The purpose of all this biological and geological tampering is "so that all may see and know . . . / that the hand of the LORD has done this" (Isa. 41:20). YHWH makes the Earth different so that humans can travel safely to Jerusalem as "home." Second Isaiah's vision is clearly anthropocentric, treating nature as a resource to serve human needs.

The vision is also far from the egalitarianism for which it is often praised. In its promises, not only the Earth but also other humans become commodities to be traded for Jacob's glory:

> I give Egypt as your ransom,
>   Cush and Seba in exchange for you.
> Because you are precious in my sight
>   and honored and I love you,
> I give people in return for you,
>   nations in exchange for your life.
>   Isa. 43:3

While it would be unfair to equate the writers of Isaiah with the ultrawealthy that Rieger describes in his critique of the "Capitalocene" era, it is nonetheless important to recognize that Second Isaiah's vision is for some and not for all.

Similarly, Second Isaiah's metaphor of Zion as the mother grieving the loss of her children is not one that benefits all equally. Although Mother Zion *is* remembered and comforted in this collection, she does not speak. She is an object of care but not a true subject, unlike Second Isaiah's male servant who voices not only his complaint but also his vindication. By characterizing the audience as Zion's lost children, ones who can console their grieving mother, this collection pulls on heartstrings tuned to patriarchal chords of motherhood. Go home, it cajoles, take care of your mother who misses you. As feminists and womanists insist, these images do not advocate for women as women but reinscribe particular stereotypes of motherhood. The same might be said of the ubiquitous trope of Mother Earth—everywhere on Earth Day—that relies on the logic of patriarchal social structures to elicit our compassion while we remain the focus of attention: even as we are called to honor our mother, she remains the one responsible for caring for us.

READING THE PROPHETS IN THE CLIMATE CRISIS

Clearly, a simple concordance search for what the Prophets say about creation and Earth is not a productive interpretive approach. Repeating the praise of God as Creator found in Genesis and Second Isaiah creation texts does little to address the modern realities of planetary devastation and the deep-seated ideologies that drive it.

Engaging these texts more deeply and honestly not only challenges unhelpful tropes but also provides more helpful pathways forward. First and most fundamentally, such engagements provide a salutary cautionary function. When Genesis and Second Isaiah are read intersectionally, paying close attention to gender and other forms of power, what is touted as good for all is revealed to privilege some over others. Even when those being privileged are themselves on lower rungs of power, advocating for their vindication can be done in ways that do not champion the needs of others equally marginalized. The same kind of self-interest and myopia often lurk beneath modern attempts at climate activism. This is true for corporate greenwashing, in which companies falsely label their products as climate friendly while doing far more to boost their sales numbers than their environmental impact. Yet it is also true for well-intentioned but relatively ineffective faith-based campaigns that urge recycling and the banning of single-use plastic bags without questioning the global economic systems that demand that goods be generated to boost the wealth of shareholders. Taking such actions may feel good but be doing little good for the planet. While proclaiming that God is doing "a new thing" (Isa. 43:19), we often leave too many "old things" unexamined.

In reading the Prophets simplistically as creation texts, we also overlook perhaps their greatest resource for the current climate crisis: the prophetic message of judgment. Judgment, of course, is not a popular topic in progressive Christianity. Progressive preachers and congregations tend to present their own message as one of love, comfort, acceptance, and forgiveness, while characterizing their counterparts in conservative Christianity as preaching fire and brimstone. Not surprisingly, progressives most commonly quote passages from Second Isaiah that offer divine comfort (Isa. 40:1–2), tell people not to fear (Isa. 40:8–10), and promise supernatural levels of protection (Isa. 43:1–2). In academic settings, textbooks and reference materials tend to present Second Isaiah as the "good stuff" following the "bad stuff" of First Isaiah's withering critique (as typified in Isa. 1).

I have argued throughout this volume that Christian appropriation of the hope of the Prophets while leaving its judgment for others is anti-Jewish. It promotes problematic stereotypes of the contrast between a wrathful Old Testament (and Jewish) God and Jesus's embodiment of the God of love. But failing to take the value of judgment seriously has other consequences as well. As this chapter has insisted, the failure to engage in appropriate judgment is harmful for the planet. This planetary moment calls not for positivity but critique.

For this reason, in this moment we may find more environmental usefulness in First Isaiah's words of judgment than in Second Isaiah's praise of God the Creator. For example, the logic of Isaiah 6 seems particularly resonant as we recognize the devastation of the planet. In Isaiah 6:9–13, the prophet is called to announce that in the present the consequences of Judah's behavior cannot be averted. Hope is possible, but only *after* the people face the harsh reality before them. Similarly, while the surrounding chapters of First Isaiah do offer words of hope, hope is presented as possible only after destruction is accomplished. I believe that this realism is vitally necessary for current climate activism: even if humans were to drastically limit their inputs into global warming (which is unlikely), some impacts of the harm we have done are likely inevitable and irreversible. We must repent of our treatment of Earth, but even repentance will not stop the consequences we must face.

A note of caution is in order, however, about simply repeating the Prophets' words of judgment in our own situation. In First Isaiah, the devastation the people are about to face is the punishment of YHWH; they have broken faith, but YHWH is the one who orchestrates the consequences. This is clear in Isaiah 24, for example, a text being increasingly used for sermons addressing climate change (Heishman 2020): "The LORD is about to lay waste the earth and make it desolate" (Isa. 24:1). In our own context, we must affirm the wisdom of the Prophets on the necessity of judgment but keep the blame squarely where it belongs: on humans, or more precisely on the people and the systems that facilitate and even normalize devastation.

Reading the Prophets, even reading them well, is not the answer to the climate crisis. We need also good science, good politics, good theology—good work all around. But good biblical interpretation is important because the Bible is being weaponized against the planet, and the harm being done in its name must be challenged. Biblical interpretation also matters because, when done with care and honesty, it has the potential for inspiring and empowering social change.

Conclusion

In all that I have written, I hope it is evident that I am committed to progressive social causes. My discussions have been grounded in gender justice, racial justice, environmental justice—justice for the Jewish faith, justice for the colonialized, and justice for the LGBTQIA community. The work of justice matters to me. It informs my scholarship and my life.

Indeed, my commitment to justice requires that I be honest about the texts I read and the perspectives from which I interpret. I find it problematic that progressives have turned the prophets of the Hebrew Bible into simple, clear reflections of their own convictions. When prophets are those who are just like us and "prophetic preaching" is indistinguishable from our own voices, we are talking far more about ourselves than about the prophetic literature of the Hebrew Bible. Given the complexity of this literature and the important insights into the ancient world that contemporary scholarship offers, it is clear that no single characterization of prophecy captures all of what these books say and do. The prophets are more and less than social critics or truth tellers or predicters or visionaries or mystics, or any other single way that we portray the prophets. Just as calling a perspective "biblical" relies on a selective reading of biblical passages and reading them through selective lenses, so too is calling a courageous stance "prophetic."

A theme that has run throughout my discussion, perhaps more important than any other, is that using the terms "prophetic" and "prophet" without any explanation or self-awareness is counterproductive in modern discourse. Not everyone uses terms about prophecy in this way, so to continue such insider-speak is confusing and arrogant, perpetuating distrust and distance between others who believe differently.

GETTING HONEST WITH OURSELVES

As the volume draws to a close, I highlight a different though related problem with this orthodoxy. It inhibits not only our understanding of others but also our recognition of the complex ways that even progressives discern truth. The language of "scientific" and "educated" obscures the complex ways in which progressives encounter the world and their faith. Even the most rational progressive reader of the Bible, who treats other views as misguided, can also express a religious sensibility in which faith and truth are not reduced to the rational.

This takes several forms. At the most basic level, progressives (like everyone else) regularly appeal to knowledge that comes through intuition or emotion. In her ethnographic study of congregations addressing the United Methodist position on homosexuality, Dawn Moon reports on the ways that both conservatives and progressives ground themselves in the realm of feeling. At times, feelings are the explanation for a position that is difficult to articulate or defend: "I can't explain it, but I know in my heart that this is true." Invoked in this way, "feelings serve as an incontestable form of knowledge" (Moon 2004, 183). We can argue about the Bible but not about the way others feel.

Moon also chronicles the ways in which progressive and conservative congregants both point to an innate sense of knowing as the basis of their ethical stances. When a course of action evokes a sense of peace or an othewise warm feeling, it is deemed faithful; when it makes someone "feel sick," it is not. Importantly, the same feeling state is reported by folks who have very different theological perspectives: a conservative might feel "settled" with a position that is quite different than the one that leaves a progressive feeling "settled" (Moon 2004, 203–4).

Of course, such feelings are themselves informed by the congregrant's prior beliefs. As both Moon and Martha Nussbaum argue, emotions are not separate from one's intellect, but instead "discrimination responses closely connected with beliefs about how things are and what is important. . . . A certain belief or beliefs at least a necessary condition for emotion" (Nussbaum 1990, 41). Yet, as Moon demonstrates, individuals are not always aware of the cognitive basis of their feelings: their experience of an emotional state itself becomes the irrefutable grounds for their decisions. That is, while *intellectual convictions* are operative for all people, progressives and conservatives at times both experience and articulate their conclusions as grounded in *emotions*. When progressives attribute an appeal to emotions as only what other less educated people do, they fail to recognize the dynamics of their own engagements.

At a deeper spiritual level, many progressive Christians embrace a faith that seeks to transcend the rational. Multitudes of Christians hold fast to the possibility of ongoing divine communication, believing or at least hoping that through prayer, preaching, study, nature, meditation, ecstatic experiences, or some combination of them, God may speak to the concerns of their world and their hearts. Their own prayer practices assume that God might not only listen but also talk back. Unlike some charismatics, they rarely use the language of "prophecy" to describe the ways in which God responds, but they nonetheless believe that reason is not the only path to divine truth.

A prime example of this prophecy-by-diverse-names dynamic comes from my own denomination, the United Church of Christ. Across the denomination's website, "prophetic" and "prophet" are equated with social justice. These terms are invoked while describing progressive stances on anti-racism, environmental justice, and LGBTQIA rights. In a statement titled "What We Believe," the terms are clearly articulated:

> We believe that the UCC is called to be a prophetic church. As in the tradition of the prophets and apostles, God calls the church to speak truth to power, liberate the oppressed, care for the poor and comfort the afflicted. (UCC n..d "What")

Such language clearly reflects the progressive orthodoxy about prophecy, one forged in the fusion of Enlightenment scholarship, Romantic sensibilities, and the Social Gospel.

Yet running throughout the same website is a strong insistence that divine revelation continues into the present. In 2004 the UCC launched a marketing campaign with the slogan "God is still speaking." The emblem was a comma, taken from a quote from the actress Gracie Allen: "Never place a period where God has placed a comma." In 2015, the identity campaign was updated to "stillspeaking 2.0." Its rollout was accompanied with provocative ad campaigns with logos such as "Revelation: God didn't end in Revelation" and "The Bible is like GPS. A brilliant guide. All-knowing. Occasionally wrong." The same statement of faith that equates "prophetic" with social justice also affirms, "We are a people of possibility. In the UCC, members, congregations and structures have the breathing room to explore and to hear . . . for after all, God is still speaking . . ." (ellipses included) (these and other graphics from the Stillspeaking 2.0 Toolkit can be found at UCC n.d.).

The claim that God is still speaking is more historically associated with charismatic Christianity. Indeed, the campaign was initiated by Ron Buford, a former Pentecostal: after attending a Jungian dream workshop and seeing Grace Allen's comma quote on a postcard, he was awakened at 3 a.m. with a vision for the campaign (Trost 2007). Yet while the language resonates with

Pentecostalism, for the UCC the claim about ongoing revelation serves to support social justice causes, especially in opposition to traditional religious views and biblical literalism. Clearly, although the UCC uses the progressive discourse for "prophetic," it leaves room for sources of knowledge other than reason, including experience.

In other Christian streams, claims of God's ongoing communication serve quite different functions. For example, the New Apostolic Reformation, a network of leaders who identify themselves as prophets and apostles, seeks to create a kingdom of God on earth—one that asserts "biblical" dominion over culture, business, and government. In a 2011 interview with Terry Gross on *Fresh Air*, a prominent leader in the movement, Peter Wagner, explained that those with other religious beliefs are demonic; rejected the legitimacy of homosexuality; and asserted that God is currently appointing apostles and prophets not only to speak to the church but to have earthly authority (NPR 2011). The movement played a major role in the 2016 election of Donald Trump and numerous attempts to overturn the results of the 2020 election.

Contrasting these two very different religious movements underscores that what distinguishes the New Apostolic Reformation from the UCC is not its claim to hear God speaking. They disagree not about *whether* God is still speaking but about what God is *actually saying*. Where the two differ—and differ dramatically—is in how they portray the *content* of the divine message.

A CALL TO HONEST AND HUMBLE ACTIVISM

It is that *content* that we should be addressing. Precisely because the stakes are so high in the modern political and religious realms (as well as their intersections), debates about how prophecy works (whether it is rational or emotional, scientific or superstituous, etc.) are far less productive than an honest and direct focus on the starkly different visions of the future currently being granted divine authority. Progressives seeking to address the challenges facing the planet and its inhabitants must be talking about the details of justice, speaking in our own voices about what environmental justice entails and why it matters to our faith, about what forms of racial justice we pursue and whose voices inform that pursuit, about how we define criminal justice, and about the basis of our convictions about gender and sexuality. We need to talk about the present and articulate what we believe is wrong while listening to others do the same.

For the work before us, we need as many partners as possible. Not only rationalist progressives but also those whom progressive discourse often alienates: for example, Evangelicals working toward LGBTQIA inclusion and climate action, and Pentecostals who advocate for justice in the global community while affirming the diverse gifts of the Spirit. I do not share all of the convictions or experiences of other Christians. The issues that divide us are real. But interpretive orthodoxies too often distract us from what is at stake, promoting polarization rather than dialogue. My hope is that our honest wrestling together about the content of our advocacy and what informs us can help us move beyond unhelpful stereotypes of one another. And when we discern that a perspective brings harm, we need more than simple orthodoxies to engage in oppositon. To simply dismiss the New Apostolic Reformation or white Christian nationalism as "uneducated" or "naïve," as many progressives do, does not equip us to resist the very real religious and political power that these understandings of prophecy are wielding in our world.

Understanding claims for and against prophecy as multifaceted and contextual challenges progressives to more fully recognize the contingent nature of what has become an uncontested interpretation. As much as many of us tout our own views as less biased and more careful than that of previous generations, we continue to be shaped by our history and our convictions. The progressive orthodoxy about the prophets does not serve us or our planet well.

Bibliography

Adair-Toteff, Christopher. 2014. "Max Weber's Charismatic Prophets." *History of the Human Sciences* 27, no. 1: 3–20.

Adams, Samuel L. n.d. "Economic Justice and the Bible." Union Theological Seminary. Accessed August 11, 2023. https://www.upsem.edu/seminarycents -practice/economic-justice-bible/.

Albani, Matthias. 2020. "Monotheism in Isaiah." In *The Oxford Handbook of Isaiah*, ed. Lena-Sofia Tiemeyer, 219–48. New York: Oxford University Press.

Alexander, Jeffrey C. 2004. "Toward a Theory of Cultural Trauma." In *Cultural Trauma and Collective Identity*, ed. Jeffrey Alexander, 1–30. Berkeley: University of California Press.

Assemblies of God. 2001. "Apostles and Prophets (Official A/G Position Paper)." General Presbytery of the Assemblies of God.

Beal, Timothy K. 2022. *When Time Is Short: Finding Our Way in the Anthropocene.* Boston: Beacon Press.

Berges, Ulrich. 2017. "Trito-Isaiah and the Reforms of Ezra/Nehemiah: Consent or Conflict?" *Biblica* 98, no. 2: 173–90. doi: 10.2143/BIB.98.2.3217841.

Bhabha, Homi K. 2004. *The Location of Culture*. London: Routledge.

Blenkinsopp, Joseph. 2006. *Opening the Sealed Book: Interpretations of the Book of Isaiah in Late Antiquity.* Grand Rapids: Eerdmans.

Brantley, W. Gasaway. 2014. *Progressive Evangelicals and the Pursuit of Social Justice.* Vol. 1. Chapel Hill: University of North Carolina Press.

Brenner, Athalya. 1996. "On 'Jeremiah' and The Poetics of (Prophetic?) Pornography." In *On Gendering Texts: Female and Male Voices in the Hebrew Bible*, by Athalya Brenner and Fokkelien van Dijk-Hemmes, 178–93. Leiden: Brill.

Brett, Mark. 2020. "Postcolonial Readings of Isaiah." In *The Oxford Handbook of Isaiah*, ed. Lena-Sofia Tiemeyer, 621–36. New York: Oxford University Press.

Bridgeman, Valerie. 2016. ""I Will Make Boys Their Princes': A Womanist Reading of Children in the Book of Isaiah." In *Womanist Interpretations of the Bible: Expanding the Discourse*, ed. Gay L. Byron and Vanessa Lovelace, 311–27. Atlanta: SBL Press.

Brown, William P. 2010. *The Seven Pillars of Creation: The Bible, Science, and the Ecology of Wonder.* Oxford: Oxford University Press.

Brunner, Daniel L., and A. J. Swoboda. 2022. "Creation Care and the Bible: An Evangelical Perspective." In *The Oxford Handbook of the Bible and Ecology*, ed. Hilary Marlow and Mark Harris, 413–24. Oxford: Oxford University Press.

Burgess, Stanley. 2011. *Christian Peoples of the Spirit: A Documentary History of Pentecostal Spirituality from the Early Church to the Present*. New York: New York University Press.

Calkins, Raymond. 1947. *The Modern Message of the Minor Prophets*. New York: Harper & Brothers.

Calvin, Jean, and Joseph Haroutunian. 1958. *Calvin: Commentaries*. Library of Christian Classics 23. Philadelphia: Westminster Press.

Carey, Greg. 2017. *Luke: An Introduction and Study Guide: All Flesh Shall See God's Salvation*. T&T Clark Study Guides to the New Testament. London: Bloomsbury T&T Clark.

Carmichael, Rodney. 2017. "The Prophetic Struggle of Kendrick Lamar's 'DAMN.'" NPR. December 12, 2017. https://www.npr.org/2017/12/12/568748405/the -prophetic-struggle-of-kendrick-lamars-damn.

Carroll R., M. Daniel. 2020. *The Book of Amos*. The New International Commentary on the Old Testament. Grand Rapids: Eerdmans.

————. 1992. *Contexts for Amos: Prophetic Poetics in Latin American Perspective*. Sheffield: JSOT Press.

Caruth, Cathy. 1996. *Unclaimed Experience: Trauma, Narrative, and History*. Baltimore: Johns Hopkins University Press.

Cataldo, Jeremiah W. 2021. "Postcolonial Approaches to the Minor Prophets." In *Oxford Handbook of the Minor Prophets*, ed. Julia M. O'Brien, 341–55. New York: Oxford University Press.

————. 2009. *A Theocratic Yehud?: Issues of Government in the Persian Period*. T&T Clark Library of Biblical Studies. New York: T&T Clark International.

Clines, David J. A. 1995. "Metacommentating Amos." In *Interested Parties: The Ideology of Writers and Readers of the Hebrew Bible*, 76–94. Sheffield: Sheffield Academic Press.

Colecchi, Stephen M. n.d. "Roots of Catholic Social Teaching Found in the Old Testament Prophets." United States Conference of Catholic Bishops. Accessed June 19, 2023. https://www.usccb.org/offices/new-american-bible/roots -catholic-social-teaching-found-old-testament-prophets.

Cone, James. (1970) 2010. *A Black Theology of Liberation: Fortieth Anniversary Edition*. Maryknoll, NY: Orbis Books. Page numbers are from the fortieth anniversary edition.

Coomber, Matthew J. M. 2010. *Re-Reading the Prophets through Corporate Globalization: A Cultural-Evolutionary Approach to Economic Injustice in the Hebrew Bible*. Piscataway, NJ: Gorgias.

Corley, Kathleen E. 2014. "Jesus." In *The Oxford Encyclopedia of the Bible and Gender Studies*, ed. Julia M. O'Brien, 391–401. New York: Oxford University Press.

Couey, J. Blake. 2021. "Amos." In *Oxford Handbook of the Minor Prophets*, ed. Julia M. O'Brien, 425–36. New York: Oxford University Press.

Cox, Roland Paul. 2019. "The Realization of Isaiah 61 in Africa." *Conspectus* 28: 120–38.

Cunningham, W. Pat. 2022. "Awake in Christ, Not Woke without Him." Sermon Central. https://www.sermoncentral.com/sermons/awake-in-christ-not-woke -without-him-w-pat-cunningham-sermon-on-prayer-266830.

Davis, Ellen F. 2009. *Scripture, Culture, and Agriculture: An Agrarian Reading of the Bible*. New York: Cambridge University Press.

Deane-Drummond, Celia, Sigurd Bergmann, and Markus Vogt, ed. 2017. *Religion in the Anthropocene*. Eugene, OR: Cascade.

de Wette, W. M. L. 1826. *The German Theological Institution in North America: Documents, Explanations, Requests.* Basel: E. Thurneisen.

Diamond, A. R. Pete. 1990. "Jeremiah's Confessions in the LXX and MT: A Witness to Developing Canonical Function?" *Vetus Testamentum* 40, no. 1: 33–50.

Doblmeier, Martin, dir. 2021. *Spiritual Audacity: The Abraham Joshua Heschel Story.* Journey Films.

Edgar, Scott. 2021. "Hermann Cohen." In *Stanford Encyclopedia of Philosophy*, ed. Edward N. Zalta. https://plato.stanford.edu/cgi-bin/encyclopedia/archinfo.cgi?entry=cohen&archive=win2022.

Elliott, George. 1910. "The Social Message of the Prophets." In *Social Ministry: An Introduction to the Study and Practice of Social Service*, ed. Harry Frederick Ward, 3–26. New York: Eaton and Mains.

Exeter Project. n.d. "Criticisms of Stewardship." University of Exeter. Accessed July 6, 2023. https://theology.exeter.ac.uk/research/projects/beyondstewardship/topics/criticisms/.

Ferguson, Mike. 2022. "Webinar Encourages Prophetic Preaching during Times of Trouble, Including Right Now." Presbyterian Church (U.S.A.). https://www.presbyterianmission.org/story/webinar-encourages-prophetic-preaching-during-times-of-trouble-including-right-now/.

Finn, Daniel K. 2013. *Christian Economic Ethics: History and Implications.* Minneapolis: Fortress.

Flippin, William E., Jr. 2012. "The Prophet Amos as a Model for Addressing Issues of Economic Justice." *HuffPost.* Sept. 15, 2012.

Force, James E. 1982. "Hume and Johnson on Prophecy and Miracles: Historical Context." *Journal of the History of Ideas* 43, no. 3: 463–75. doi: 10.2307/2709433.

Fosdick, Harry Emerson. 1938. *A Guide to Understanding the Bible: The Development of Ideas within the Old and New Testaments.* New York: Harper & Brothers.

———. 1936. "Christian Attitudes in Social Reconstruction." In *Papers of Harry Emerson Fosdick.* Union Theological Seminary.

———. 1933. "Plea for Genuine Individualism." In *Papers of Harry Emerson Fosdick.* Union Theological Seminary.

Francis (Pope). 2015. *Laudato Si'.* Encyclical of the Holy See. https://www.vatican.va/content/francesco/en/encyclicals/documents/papa-francesco_20150524_enciclica-laudato-si.html.

Frankl, Viktor. 1985. *Man's Search for Meaning.* New York: Simon and Schuster.

Fund Our Schools. 2021. "Why We Are in Court: Key Facts about School Funding in PA." Education Law Center PA. https://www.fundourschoolspa.org/resources.

Gafney, Wilda. 2017. *Nahum, Habakkuk, Zephaniah.* Wisdom Commentary Series. Collegeville, MN: Liturgical.

Gehr, Chris. 2016. "Following Up: Micah 6:8 in American Rhetoric." *The Pietest Schoolman.* https://pietistschoolman.com/2016/07/28/following-up-micah-68-in-american-rhetoric/.

Gieryn, Thomas. 1983. "Boundary-Work and the Demarcation of Science from Non-Science: Strains and Interests in Professional Ideologies of Scientists." *American Sociological Review* 6: 78–795.

Grinspoon, David. 2016. *The Earth in Human Hands: Shaping our Planet's Future.* New York: Grand Central Publishing.

Gutiérrez, Gustavo. 1988. *A Theology of Liberation: 15th Anniversary Edition*. Maryknoll, NY: Orbis Books. Originally published as *Teología de la liberación* (Lima: CEP, 1971). Page numbers are from the fifteenth anniversary edition.

Hanson, Paul D. 1995. *Isaiah 40–66*. Louisville, KY: Westminster John Knox Press.

Heishman, Tim. 2020. "A Reflection on Isaiah 24:4–6: Climate Justice." Church of the Brethren. brethren.org/news/2020/reflection-on-isaiah-climate-justice.

Henderson, Joe. 2019. *Jeremiah under the Shadow of Duhm: A Critique of the Use of Poetic Form as a Criterion of Authenticity*. London: T&T Clark.

Henry, Matthew. n.d. "Matthew Henry's Concise Commentary." Accessed August 11, 2023. https://biblehub.com/commentaries/micah/2-2.htm.

Herman, Judith. 1997. *Trauma and Recovery: The Aftermath of Violence—from Domestic Abuse to Political Terror*. New York: Basic Books.

Heschel, Susannah. 2008. *The Aryan Jesus: Christian Theologians and the Bible in Nazi Germany*. Princeton, NJ: Princeton University Press.

Higginbottom, Ryan. 2020. "Context Matters: Do Justice, Love Mercy, Walk Humbly with God." *Knowable Word*. https://www.knowableword.com/2020/11/23/context-matters-do-justice-love-mercy-walk-humbly-with-god/.

Hillers, Delbert. 1984. *Micah*. Philadelphia: Fortress.

Houston, Walter J. 2008. *Contending for Justice: Ideologies and Theologies of Social Justice in the Old Testament*. Paperback edition. New York: T & T Clark.

———. n.d. "Social Justice and the Prophets." *Bible Odyssey*. Accessed September 2, 2022. https://www.bibleodyssey.org/articles/social-justice-and-the-prophets/.

Howard, Thomas A. 2000. *Religion and the Rise of Historicism: W. M. L. de Wette, Jacob Burckhardt, and the Theological Origins of Nineteenth-Century Historical Consciousness*. Cambridge, UK: Cambridge University Press.

IPCC. 2023. "Headline Statements." https://www.ipcc.ch/report/ar6/syr/resources/spm-headline-statements/.

Jefferson, Lauren. 2017. "Forging Peace: 'Guns into Plowshares' Sculpture Dedicated at EMU." Eastern Mennonite University. https://emu.edu/now/news/2017/forging-peace-guns-plowshares-sculpture-dedicated-emu/.

Jennings, Willie James 2020. *After Whiteness: An Education in Belonging*. Grand Rapids: Eerdmans.

Jewish Daily Bulletin. 1927. "Dr. Fosdick Sees Danger for Zionism; Objects to Political Feature." *Jewish Daily Bulletin*, May 20.

Kay, William K. 2011. *Pentecostalism: A Very Short Introduction*. New York: Oxford University Press.

Kessler, Rainer. 2021. "Micah." In *Oxford Handbook of the Minor Prophets*, edited by Julia M. O'Brien, 461–71. New York: Oxford University Press.

Kolbert, Elizabeth. 2021. "How Politics Got So Polarized." *The New Yorker*, December 27. https://www.newyorker.com/magazine/2022/01/03/how-politics-got-so-polarized.

Kraemer, Ross S. 1985. "Book Review: In Memory of Her." Review of *In Memory of Her: A Feminist Theological Reconstruction of Christian Origins* by Elisabeth Schussler Fiorenza. *Journal of Biblical Literature* 104, no. 4: 722–25.

Kuenen, Abraham. 1877. *The Prophets and Prophecy in Israel*. Translated by Adam Milroy. London: Longmans, Green, and Co.

Kung, Hans. 2007. "The Prophetic Jesus." In *Living the Questions*. Bible Study Curriculumsession 9. DVD Curriculum.

Kurtz, Paul Michael. 2022. Personal email communication with the author. Sept. 9, 2022.

———. 2021. "Is Kant among the Prophets? Hebrew Prophecy and German Historical Thought, 1880–1920." *Central European History* 54.

———. 2019. "The Silence on the Land: Ancient Israel versus Modern Palestine in Scientific Theology." In *Negotiating the Secular and the Religious in the German Empire*, edited by Rebekka Habermas, 56–97. New York: Berghahn.

———. 2018. *Kaiser, Christ, and Canaan: The Religion of Israel in Protestant Germany, 1871–1918*. Forschungen zum Alten Testament 122. Tübingen: Mohr Siebeck.

———. 2016. "Waiting at Nemi: Wellhausen, Gunkel, and the World behind Their Work." *Harvard Theological Review* 109, no. 4: 567–85.

Leese, J. J. Johnson. 2019. "Ecofaith: Reading Scripture in an Era of Ecological Crisis." *Religions* 10(3), no. 154. https://doi.org/10.3390/rel10030154.

Leonhardt, David. 2023. "The Politics of Class." *New York Times*, June 22.

Levine, Amy-Jill. 2019. "The Gospels and Acts." In *The Oxford Handbook of New Testament, Gender, and Sexuality*, ed. Benjamin H. Dunning, 295–314. New York: Oxford University Press.

———. 2007. *The Misunderstood Jew: The Church and the Scandal of the Jewish Jesus*. San Francisco: Harper One.

Lias, J. J., ed. 1892. *Cambridge Greek Testament for School and Colleges*. Cambrige: University Press.

Macwilliam, Stuart. 2002. "Queering Jeremiah." *Biblical Interpretation* 10: 384–404.

Martin, Craig. 2009. "How to Read an Interpretation: Interpretive Strategies and the Maintenance of Authority." *The Bible and Critical Theory* 5, no. 1: 6.1–6.26.

McKenzie, Steven L. 2009. *How to Read the Bible: History, Prophecy, Literature—Why Modern Readers Need to Know the Difference and What It Means for Faith Today*. New York: Oxford University Press.

Melcher, Sarah J. 2007. "With Whom Do the Disabled Associate? Metaphorical Interplay in the Latter Prophets. " In *This Abled Body: Rethinking Disabilities in Biblical Studies*, ed. Hector Avalos et al., 115–29. Atlanta: Society of Biblical Literature.

Micah Movement. 2023. "The Micah Movement." https://micahmovement.com.

Micah Project. n.d. "Micah Project." Who We Are / About Us. Accessed August 14, 2023. https://micahprojecthonduras.org/who-we-are/about-us.html.

Middlemas, Jill Anne. 2011. "Trito-Isaiah's Intra- and Internationalization: Identity Markers in the Second Temple Period." In *Judah and the Judeans in the Achaemenid Period: Negotiating Identity in an International Context*, ed. Oded Lipschits et al., 105–25. Winona Lake, IN: Eisenbrauns.

Miller, Robert. 1985. *Harry Emerson Fosdick: Preacher, Prophet, Pastor*. New York: Oxford University Press.

Moon, Dawne. 2004. *God, Sex, and Politics: Homosexuality and Everyday Theologies*. Chicago: University of Chicago Press.

Morris, Gerald. 1996. *Prophecy, Poetry and Hosea*. Sheffield: Sheffield Academic Press.

Muir, J. 1877. "Introduction." In *The Prophets and Prophecy in Israel*, ix–xl. London: Longmans, Green, and Co.

NASA. n.d. "Do Scientists Agree on Climate Change?" NASA. Accessed July 5, 2023. https://climate.nasa.gov/faq/17/do-scientists-agree-on-climate-change/.

Nasrallah, Laura Salah. 2003. *An Ecstasy of Folly: Prophecy and Authority in Early Christianity*. Harvard Theological Studies 52. Cambridge, MA: Harvard University Press.

National Conference of Catholic Bishops. 1986. *Economic Justice for All: Pastoral Letter on Catholic Social Teaching and the U.S. Economy.* Office of Publishing and Promotion Services, United States Catholic Conference, no. 101. Washington, DC: U.S. Catholic Conference.

National Council of Congregational Churches. 1907. *Addresses and Discussions of Thirteenth Triennial Session of the National Council of Congregational Churches.* Boston: Office of the Secretary of the General Council.

Nicoll, William Robertson, ed. 1900. *The Sermon Bible: Isaiah to Malachi.* Vol. 4. New York: Funk & Wagnalls.

NPR. 2011. "A Leading Figure in the New Apostolic Reformation." *Fresh Air.* https://www.npr.org/2011/10/03/140946482/apostolic-leader-weighs-religions-role-in-politics.

Nussbaum, Martha. 1990. *Love's Knowledge: Essays on Philosophy and Literature.* New York: Oxford University Press.

O'Brien, Julia M. 2022. "Forthtellers Not Foretellers: The Origins of a Liberal Orthodoxy about the Prophets." *Religions* 13, no. 4. doi: 10.3390/rel13040298.

———. 2015. *Micah.* Wisdom Commentary Series. Collegeville, MN: Liturgical Press.

———. 2008. *Challenging Prophetic Metaphor: Theology and Ideology in the Prophets.* Louisville, KY: Westminster John Knox Press.

———. 2002. *Nahum.* Sheffield: Sheffield Academic Press.

O'Connor, Kathleen. 2011. *Jeremiah: Pain and Promise.* Minneapolis: Fortress.

———. 2010. "Reclaiming Jeremiah's Violence." In *The Aesthetics of Violence in the Prophets*, ed. Chris Franke and Julia M. O'Brien, 37–49. New York: T&T Clark.

Oden, Amy G. 2011. "Commentary on Micah 6:1–8." Luther Seminary. https://www.workingpreacher.org/commentaries/revised-common-lectionary/fourth-sunday-after-epiphany/commentary-on-micah-61-8.

Pak, G. Sujin. 2018. *The Reformation of Prophecy: Early Modern Interpretations of the Prophet and Old Testament Prophecy.* Oxford Studies in Historical Theology. New York: Oxford University Press.

Plaskow, Judith. 1978. "Christian Feminism and Anti-Judaism." *Cross Currents* 28, no. 3: 306–9.

Premnath, D. N. 2003. *Eighth-Century Prophets: A Social Analysis.* St. Louis: Chalice.

Raphael, Rebecca. 2011. "Whoring after Cripples: On the Intersection of Gender and Disability Imagery in Jeremiah." In *Disability Studies and Biblical Literature*, ed. Candida R. Moss and Jeremy Schipper, 103–16. New York: Palgrave Macmillan.

Rauschenbusch, Walter. 1914. *Dare We Be Christians?* Boston: Pilgrim Press.

———. 1907. *Christianity and the Social Crisis.* London: Macmillan.

Reed, Annette. 2017. "Writing Jewish Astronomy in the Early Hellenistic Age: The Enochic Astronomical Book as Aramaic Wisdom and Archival Impulse." *Dead Sea Discoveries* 24:1–37.

Rieger, Joerg. 2022. *Theology in the Capitalocene: Ecology, Identity, Class, and Solidarity, Dispatches.* Minneapolis: Fortress.

Rosalez, Ruben. 2023. "The Exploitation of Garment Workers: Threading the Needle on Fast Fashion." *U.S. Department of Labor Blog.* https://blog.dol.gov/2023/03/21/the-exploitation-of-garment-workers-threading-the-needle-on-fast-fashion.

Runions, Erin. 2001. *Changing Subjects: Gender, Nation, and Future in Micah.* London: Sheffield Academic Press.

Said, Edward W. 1979. *Orientalism*. 1st Vintage Books ed. New York: Vintage Books.

Sanderson, Judith. 1992. "Amos." In *The Women's Bible Commentary*, ed. Carol A. Newsom and Sharon H. Ringe, 205–9. London and Louisville: SPCK and Westminster John Knox Press.

Sasson, Jack M. 1995. "Water beneath Straw: Adventures of a Prophetic Phrase in the Mari Archives." In *Solving Riddles and Untying Knots: Biblical, Epigraphic, and Semitic Studies in Honor of James C Greenfield*, ed. Ziony Zevit et al., 599–608. Winona Lake, IN: Eisenbrauns.

Schipper, Jeremy. 2011. *Disability and Isaiah's Suffering Servant, Biblical Refigurations*. Oxford: Oxford University Press.

Schultz, Erika. 2013. "Seattle's Landesa Aims to Help Rural Girls in India." *Seattle Times*, March 17. https://www.seattletimes.com/photo-video/photography/seattles-landesa-aims-to-help-rural-girls-in-india/.

Sharp, Carolyn J. 2021. *Jeremiah 26–52*. International Exegetical Commentary on the Old Testament. Stuttgart: Kohlhammer.

———. 2009. *Irony and Meaning in the Hebrew Bible*. Indiana Studies in Biblical Literature. Bloomington: Indiana University Press.

Sheehan, Jonathan. 2005. *The Enlightenment Bible: Translation, Scholarship, Culture*. Princeton, NJ: Princeton University Press.

Simmons, Fred. 2019. "From Alarm to Autopsy: Climate Change and the Role of Death in Contemporary Christian Hope." Paper presented to the AAR annual meeting, November 23, San Diego, CA.

Smith, Mitzi. 2016. "Race, Gender, and the Politics of 'Sass': Reading Mark 7:24–30 through a Womanist Lens of Intersectionality and Inter(con)textuality." In *Womanist Interpretations of the Bible: Expanding the Discourse*, ed. Gay L. Byron and Vanessa Lovelace, 95–112. Atlanta: SBL Press.

Smith, Stephen. 2023. "95 Bible Verses about the Preferential Option for the Poor and Vulnerable." OpenBible.info. https://www.openbible.info/topics/preferential_option_for_the_poor_and_vulnerable.

Smith, W. Robertson. 1882. *The Prophets of Israel and Their Place in History to the Close of the 8th Century B.C.* Edinburgh: Adam and Charles Black.

Smith-Christopher, Daniel L. 2021. "The Problem of 'Justice' as Social Criticism in the Twelve Prophets." In *The Oxford Handbook of the Minor Prophets*, ed. Julia M. O'Brien, 159–72. New York: Oxford University Press.

Spivak, Gayatri. 1988. "Can the Subaltern Speak?" In *Marxism and the Interpretation of Culture*, edited by Cary Nelson and Lawrence Grossberg, 271–313. Urbana: University of Illinois Press.

Stökl, Jonathan. 2015. "Prophetic Hermeneutics in the Hebrew Bible and Mesopotamia." *Hebrew Bible and Ancient Israel* 4, no. 3: 267–92. doi: 10.1628/219222715 X14507102280810.

Strong, James. 1890. "*Prophetes* (Gk)." In *Exhaustive Concordance of the Bible*. Online at https://biblehub.com/greek/4396.htm.

Stulman, Louis. 2018. "Jeremiah." In *New Oxford Annotated Bible*, 5th ed., ed. Michael Coogan, et al., 1069–61. New York: Oxford University Press.

Swords to Ploughshares. n.d. "About Us." Accessed August 15, 2023. https://www.swords-to-plowshares.org/.

Swords to Plowshares Northeast. n.d. "About Us." Accessed August 15, 2023. https://www.s2pnortheast.org/about.

Tabbernee, William. 2007. *Fake Prophecy and Polluted Sacraments: Ecclesiastical and Imperial Reactions to Montanism*. Supplements to Vigiliae Christianae. Leiden: Brill.

Taylor, Jeremy. 1647. "The Liberty of Prophesying." In *Treatises*. London: Royston. http://name.umdl.umich.edu/A64135.0001.001.

Tisdale, Leonora Tubbs. 2010. *Prophetic Preaching: A Pastoral Approach*. Louisville, KY: Westminster John Knox Press.

Trevett, Christine. 1996. *Montanism: Gender, Authority, and the New Prophecy*. New York: Cambridge University Press.

Trost, Theodore Louis. 2007. "Identity and Identification: The United Church of Christ's 'God is still speaking' Television Ad Campaign." *Prism* 21, no. 2: 102–22.

True, David, ed. 2021. *Prophecy in a Secular Age: An Introduction*. Eugene, OR: Pickwick Publications.

Turner, Mary Donovan. 2008. "Prophetic Preaching." In *The New Interpreter's Handbook of Preaching*, ed. Paul Scott Wilson, 101–3. Nashville: Abingdon Press.

UCC. 2009. "Ministering to Those Struggling and Suffering in the Troubled Economy." Resolution of the 27th General Synod of the United Church of Christ.

———. n.d. "Stillspeaking 2.0 Toolkit." Accessed March 18, 2024. https://www.ucc.org/about/stillspeaking-2-0-toolkit/.

———. n.d. "What We Believe." Accessed August 26, 2023. https://www.ucc.org/what-we-believe.

Uwaegbute, Kingsley Ikechukwu. 2019. "A Social-Scientific Reading of Luke 4:16–19 and the Problem of Ethnic Minorities in Nigeria." *Neotestamentica* 53, no. 1: 101–21.

van der Kolk, Bessel A. 2014. *The Body Keeps the Score: Brain, Mind, and Body in the Healing of Trauma*. New York: Viking.

von Rad, Gerhard. 1965. *Old Testament Theology*. Trans. D. M. G. Stalker. 2 vols. New York: Harper & Row.

Washington, Harold C. 1997. "Violence and the Construction of Gender in the Hebrew Bible: A New Historicist Approach." *Biblical Interpretation* 5, no. 4: 324–63.

Watkins, Pat. 2021. "Toolkit for Launching Your Creation Care Ministry." United Methodist Church. https://www.umcdiscipleship.org/resources/resources-for-creation-care.

Weber, Max. [1968]. 1978. *Economy and Society: An Outline of Interpretive Sociology*. Berkeley: University of California Press. Page numbers refer to the University of California edition.

———. 1952. *Ancient Judaism*. Trans. Hans Gerth and Don Martindale. Glencoe, IL: Free Press.

Weems, Renita. 1995. *Battered Love: Marriage, Sex, and Violence in the Hebrew Prophets*. Minneapolis: Augsburg Fortress.

Wellhausen, Julius. [1881] 1973. *Prolegomena to the History of Ancient Israel; with a reprint of the Article Israel from the Encyclopaedia Britannica*. Gloucester, MA: Peter Smith. Page numbers refer to the Peter Smith edition.

White, Lynn. 1967. "The Historical Roots of our Ecologic Crisis." *Science* 155: 1203–7.

Wikipedia. n.d. "Swords to Ploughshares." Accessed August 15, 2023. https://en.wikipedia.org/wiki/Swords_to_ploughshares.

Williamson, Clark. 1982. *Has God Rejected His People? Anti-Judaism in the Christian Church*. Nashville: Abingdon Press.

World Council of Churches. 2022. *Called to Transformation: Ecumenical Diakonia.* https://
www.oikoumene.org/resources/publications/ecumenical-diakonia.

World Economic Forum. 2020. "What Is Environmental Racism and How Can We
Fight It?" World Economic Forum. https://www.weforum.org/agenda/2020
/07/what-is-environmental-racism-pollution-covid-systemic/.

Yates, Kyle Monroe. 1942. *Preaching from the Prophets.* New York: Harper & Brothers.

Yoder, John Howard. 2020. "John Howard Yoder on the Church as Witness to Peace."
James Luther Adams Foundation. https://jameslutheradams.org/the-church
-as-witness-to-peace/.

Zapff, Burkard M. 2017. "Why Is Micah Similar to Isaiah?" *Zeitschrift für die Alttesta-
mentliche Wissenschaft* 129, no. 4: 536–54. doi: 10.1515/zaw-2017-4008.

———. *Micah.* International Exegetical Commentary on the Old Testament. Stuttgart: Kohlhammer.

Zevit, Ziony. 2004. "The Prophet vs. Priest Antagonism Hypothesis: Its History and
Origin." In *The Priests in the Prophets: The Portrayal of Priests, Prophets, and Other Religious Specialists in the Latter Prophets*, ed. Lester L. Grabbe and Alice Ogden Bellis,
189–217. London: Bloomsbury.

Scripture Index

Author Index

Subject Index